
HIGHSMITH 45-220

A CRITIQUE OF
PARADISE LOST

A CRITIQUE OF
Paradise Lost

JOHN PETER

ARCHON BOOKS
1970

ISBN: 0-208-00991-4
Library of Congress Catalog Number: 70-121758
Printed in the United States of America

TO MY COLLEAGUES
AT RHODES AND AT MANITOBA

καὶ μὲν τοῖσιν ἐγὼ μεθομίλεον ἐκ Πύλου ἐλθών,
τηλόθεν ἐξ ἀπίης γαίης

CONTENTS

PREFACE

This book was prepared and written during a year spent as Hugh Le May Fellow at Rhodes University in South Africa. My warmest thanks are due to the Humanities Research Council of Canada for an award which first enabled me to undertake the work, to the electors to the Hugh Le May Fellowship, and to individuals at Rhodes who helped me along the way. I am especially grateful to Professor Guy Butler and Professor Kenneth White; to Professor David Burnett and Professor J. A. Gledhill; to Rhodes' librarians, Dr. F. G. van der Riet and Mr. R. A. Brown; and to Professor R. K. J. E. Antonissen, who checked my translations from Vondel.

The indebtedness of any writer on *Paradise Lost* must be vast and unspecifiable, but I should like to record a special debt to A. J. A. Waldock's *Paradise Lost and Its Critics*, a book which seems to me second only to the text itself for a true understanding of the critical problems posed by the poem. Re-reading it I have wondered whether the agreements between it and some of my own chapters might not have passed the point where such things cease to be comforting and become an embarrassment. But if a critical verdict is sound it will usually bear repeating from a different point of view; and this is particularly true in a climate of disagreement such as Miltonic studies at present provide.

J.D.P.

Chapter One

PROLOGUE

A REMARKABLE note written on the fly-leaves of one of his books, Warton's edition of Milton's *Poems Upon Several Occasions*, reflects Coleridge's unwillingness, as a critic, to find fault with the volume's contents.[1] 'Of criticism', it declares, 'we may perhaps say, that those divine poets, Homer, Eschylus, and the two compeers, Dante, Shakespeare, Spenser, Milton, who deserve to have Critics, κριταί, are placed above criticism in the vulgar sense, and move in the sphere of religion, while those who are not such scarcely deserve criticism in any sense.' Having in effect thus boldly disposed of all criticism, of major and minor writers alike, the most thoughtful of English critics goes on to declare that, 'speaking generally, it is far, far better to distinguish poetry into different classes; and, instead of fault-finding, to say this belongs to such or such a class—thus noting inferiority in the *sort* rather than censure on the particular poem or poet'. Criticism, all but dismissed and now in addition reduced to classification, suffers a final rebuff when he concludes by pointing out that its real purpose is not to judge but to isolate merits and praise them. 'In short, the wise is the genial; and the genial judgement is to distinguish accurately the character and characteristics of each poem, praising them according to their force and vivacity in their own kind—and to reserve reprehension for such as have no *character*— tho' the wisest reprehension would be not to speak of them at all.'

The passage illustrates very well the difficulty of generalizing about the critic's activity, and it is easy enough to refute Coleridge's assertions in it by setting them over against his own critical practice, showing for instance how his concluding injunction to

---

[1] *Coleridge's Miscellaneous Criticism*, ed. T. M. Raysor (London, 1936), p. 170.

taciturnity is betrayed by a marginal note later in the same volume, which censures the first sixty lines of 'Il Penseroso' for being 'such as many a second-rate poet, a pygmy compared with Milton, might have written'. Its real interest, however, lies less in its revelation of a superb mind momentarily perplexed than in the submerged idea of trespass it conveys, the sense of criticism as essentially hostile and derogatory. This is a common attitude, surviving and reasserting itself from age to age, and it intensifies in proportion with the eminence of the author whose work is criticized. In our own time we have seen Dr. F. R. Leavis reproved and occasionally reviled for his uncompromising assessment of Milton's verse, and the late A. J. A. Waldock obliged to moderate his criticisms of *Paradise Lost* lest they should prove too unpalatable.[1] The literary conservatism which mistrusts or derides adverse criticism of an established reputation has been much in evidence in discussions of *Paradise Lost*, and for all its excesses it cannot be simply ignored. No doubt at its worst it shows all the arrogance of insecurity. Still, at its best it springs from a commendable humility, a revulsion against that kind of patronage of the great made popular by Lytton Strachey. It is not that Dr. Leavis, for example, has anything in common with Strachey, whose methods he may fairly be said to detest. But to a disengaged and perhaps inattentive mind, especially a generous one, any attempt to probe the weaknesses in Milton's work may seem ungrateful, if only because particular adverse judgements are easily misunderstood, by the ignorant or ill-disposed, and misapplied to justify, or even construed as, a rejection of everything the poet ever wrote.

Abusus non tollit usum. From such misrepresentation no critic can effectively preserve himself, nor should he try. But he ought to be prepared to defend his stringency against the objections which a more indulgent reader might advance, if only to absolve himself from the stigma of iconoclasm. Perhaps for this purpose no more is needed than a reminder of the diverse purposes which literary

---

[1] See F. R. Leavis, *The Common Pursuit* (London, 1952), p. 32 n.

criticism can properly serve. Surely our sense of dissatisfied comment on Milton's poetry as a presumptuous trespass is justified
only so long as we interpret the function of criticism primarily in
relation to the poet himself, conceding (like Coleridge in the
passage quoted) that the critic's chief task is merely to furnish
judicious tributes to Milton's artistry, a form of homage, or to
withhold them when he cannot. So considered, criticism can only
be appreciative, for if it is less the critic must be seen as claiming,
by implication, his personal superiority to a poet whom three
centuries of readers have admired. There is, however, another
point of view, and one that does not lack authoritative endorse-
ment. To attribute it to Coleridge may be difficult, in view of the
infrequency with which he adopted it, but to two other great
critics, Johnson and Arnold, it was the very essence of a critic's
function, as natural as the flight of birds. Here criticism is related,
not so much to the subject of inquiry, the poet, but to the reader
of poet and critic alike, that 'common reader' to whom both
Johnson and Arnold instinctively appealed, to whom the judicial
critic must perforce appeal, however unpropitious the signs of
ever locating him. On this view the question of homage is
irrelevant. The critic's aim instead is to stimulate and challenge
the reader's habits in reading, providing object lessons, in so far as
he can, of how—and how not—to read, so that ultimately his
criticism may be empowered to form and define, in the actual
practice of appealing to it, the literary taste and judgement of his
time. This may be a large endeavour; it is not in any sense a dis-
creditable one. Such a critic, breaking through into apparent
heresy in his pursuit of honest judgement, can take comfort from
Coleridge's statement that 'the very act of dissenting from established opinions must generate habits precursive to the love of freedom', and from Milton's own insistence on the need for practical
wisdom, 'not to know at large of things remote From use,
obscure and suttle', and for a certain hard-headedness in one's
reading, a readiness to challenge and reject.[1] 'I think one pays a

---

[1] *Inquiring Spirit*, ed. Kathleen Coburn (London, 1951), p. 91; *P.L.* viii. 188–97,
P.R. iv. 322–30.

better compliment to the object of one's admiration', Somerset Maugham once wrote, 'when one considers him with sense than when one surrenders oneself to him like a drunkard to his glass of gin.'[1] Milton might have phrased this less flippantly, with the full emphasis of his mind and character, but the sentiment is his. Moreover he, like Johnson and Arnold in their turn, was far less concerned for any individual 'object of admiration' than for the public at large, the audience to whom his poems and pamphlets were addressed. There seems to be no real objection, then, to writing about his *Paradise Lost* as attentively, as discriminatingly, and as candidly as one can.

There is another point which a critic of *Paradise Lost* may feel obliged to emphasize, one which can best be made in terms of the work of some author other than Milton himself. I choose for this purpose a speech in the *Adam in Ballingschap* of Joost van den Vondel, Milton's Dutch contemporary, a comparable poet whose work will be referred to from time to time in the succeeding chapters of this book. It is the speech in Act Four with which Adam removes himself from the stage, leaving Eve alone in the garden where at once Belial accosts her and tempts her to eat of the forbidden fruit. Up to this point in the Act the dialogue of Adam and Eve has been a continuous ecstatic paean, first in praise of the celestial city God has created 'in the light overhead', finally in praise of the human love which their nuptials have symbolized. Adam has appealed to his bride to be as fruitful as she is loving, supplying and decorating the empty earth with as many incarnate souls as there are flowers to bedeck the fields. She replies with simple modesty that her love for him will never falter:

> As long as earth hangs in the arm of heaven
> And like a bride takes her fertility
> From such a bridegroom, who with his thousand eyes
> Of stars adores her from the arch of the sky,
> Just so long will my love be matched with yours,
> Your kindness and your kisses be returned.

---

[1] *A Writer's Notebook* (London, 1951), p. 131.

To which Adam in turn replies:

> Grant me permission to go apart a little
> Close by, to speak awhile with the Creator
> Alone, to thank him for his gift of you.
> Pardon me a moment.[1]

Now this reply of Adam's can be regarded in two quite different ways, depending on the interests of the auditor or reader confronted with it. To one sort of reader or theatregoer it is bound to seem a very clumsy device for getting Adam out of Belial's way, and altogether out of key with the ninety-odd lines of dialogue preceding it. Why should Adam make this abrupt and seemingly fortuitous decision to withdraw? And why should he make it at a juncture so convenient and yet unsuitable? Though expressing himself through questions like these this sort of witness is actually not much interested in the answers to them. His concern is not with the reasons why Vondel should have introduced the speech, but with its dramatic and aesthetic effect as it stands, its appropriateness or inappropriateness at this particular moment in the play. Trying to explain his sense of its inadequacy he will relate it to the opening lines of the Act in which it occurs, where Eve expresses an ecstatic longing to cast aside the trammels of her humanity and to escape into the life of the spirit, while Adam restrains and calms her:

Eve.	The divine music of the bridal song
	Unties the strings tethering soul to body.
	The soul, craving celestial intercourse,
	Breaks free of earth and turns to purest flame,
	Seeking the source from which its being came.
Adam.	Whither my love? Wait, you must not escape me.
Eve.	Some force drives me towards that holy fountain
	And it alone can quench me. Let me go.
Adam.	Your natural sphere is here. Your lover appeals to you.
Eve.	And now I come to myself again, to my senses.[2]

After a passage like this, our first witness will say, it is surely to

---

[1] See passage A in the Appendix.   [2] Passage B in the Appendix.

risk the appearance of hypocrisy in Adam—to say nothing of indifference—when he is made to turn on Eve with his 'Pardon me a moment', at once withdrawing to commune *in eenzaemheit* with God. If we remember the corresponding separation in Book Nine of *Paradise Lost*, the scrupulous stages by which Milton brings his Eve to her vulnerable solitude, our reaction to the speech will be even more dissatisfied. The separation can be managed, but not like this.

Another sort of reader or theatregoer, more intent on Vondel's meaning than on the critical assessment of what he wrote, and more of a scholar than the first, will find the speech quite easy to accept. He will be familiar with editorial and expository comments on the speech, and will be able to point out that Vondel's intention was actually to show how, under the stress of ecstasy, the human soul is forced to turn away from its fellow-souls, however deeply loved, to seek in solitude a direct and mystical communion with its Creator. Vondel's insight, he will say, is masterly: 'Man cannot endure his bliss; in moments of supreme grief and supreme happiness he has to turn to solitude.'[1] Eve's ready acceptance of Adam's departure ('My dearest, go with God', she says) implies no readiness on her part to be neglected, but is simply an admission that this is so. She is herself the occasion of Adam's happiness, its efficient cause, but to appreciate it truly he must ignore her, directing his thanks to that First Cause which endowed him with the capacity to feel it in the first place. So much is condensed into Adam's four lines. They are not abrupt but merely concentrated.

It is a common assumption, in the face of two interpretations of this kind, that the first is premature and that the second has disposed of it. But the real truth is that the first is irrefutable, and that the second has only arisen because some palliation of the poet's fault was necessary. The first comment is that of the critic proper, a witness whose attention must be concentrated, with all the fidelity and sense of relevance he can muster, on what may be

---

[1] Cyriel Verschaeve, *Vondel's Trilogie* (Brugge, 1941), p. 156, translated.

said to be objectively there in the sample he is examining. For him, the sample before him can only be the sum of its effects, not its intentions: those effects which are accessible to every sensitive reader or theatregoer, and which have consequently a pragmatic claim to being called objective. This is the only dependable way of assessing a piece of literature, for if the artist's intentions are assumed to enter into the assessment a critic will soon find himself trying to appraise a phantom, the poem or play or story as it might or should have been, not as it is. Such a phantom, inconspicuous but perceptible, is precisely what our second witness has introduced. In explaining why Vondel came to write Adam's speech in the form it has he has stealthily or inadvertently distracted attention from its demerits, in effect substituting for it another and fuller speech from which these demerits have been removed. The ease with which such a substitution can be made renders criticism peculiarly exacting. Having examined a passage for what it is conveying, not for what it was meant to convey, we often find that there is some incongruity or disturbance in it, some defect of presentation or phrasing which throws the objective effect out of kelter. If our approach is to avoid pusillanimity and incompleteness it is then often necessary to account for the incongruity, to explain the writer's oversight as plausibly as we can. The treatment meted out by Milton to his supermundane figures requires just this kind of analysis, as later chapters of this book will try to show. But the analysis must be strictly limited to explanation; justification lies beyond its scope. The evaluative process can only operate on what is already there in the text, and to stretch it into subjectivities of motive and intention is to becloud and confuse it. The point is crucial in literary criticism and yet many critics, I think critics of Milton's poetry in particular, habitually slide over it. A work like *Paradise Lost* raises endless questions of intention like this one in Vondel's play, and once allowed to intrude they easily come between us and the substance of the poem.

In brief what I am saying then is this: that any critic trying to deal with Milton's epic has one important obligation and one important privilege. He must work with as close a sense of relevance as he can, proceeding always from what seems to be actually present in the poem. And he is entitled to have his findings sensibly considered, without alarm or cursory hostility. To those who feel that these are axioms of criticism which might have been taken for granted my reply must be that in the past their status as axioms has been largely ignored.

Chapter Two

GOD AND HIS ANGELS

Goद and his angels ('his' may be left uncapitalized since this is a character in a poem) are not directly present in Books One and Two, yet certain passages there anticipate the treatment later accorded them. For our initial assumptions about the inhabitants of Heaven we are dependent less on particular passages than on the general implications latent in the presentation of Satan and his army. The fallen angels are meant to overawe us, and they do, but nothing said of them can discount the fact that they have been defeated. A natural disposition thus exists to think of their opponent, God, as the embodiment of perfect strength and majesty, and of their uncorrupted fellow-angels as paragons. Certain passages maintain this disposition. What is more significant is that some do not. The result, even at this stage, is to shade or faintly qualify the notions of heavenly perfection we have been entertaining.

When Satan demands

> But what power of mind
> Foreseeing or presaging, from the Depth
> Of knowledge past or present, could have fear'd,
> How such united force of Gods, how such
> As stood like these, could ever know repulse? (i. 626-30)

we share his incredulity and our own 'power of mind' is baffled by God's might. When Belial concedes that God is both omnipotent and omniscient, and calls the fallen angels' plotting 'vain' (ii. 188-98), he seems more perceptive and convincing than the other devils. Yet he also attributes to God exasperation and 'rage' (143-4), and vindictive 'anger' (158-9), together with an inclination to deride (191). Predisposed, as we are, to think of God as ineffably majestic our reaction is to reject his comments as slanderous, but they are emphatic enough to leave a suppressed mistrust which later passages are free to reawaken. Nor is this mistrust diminished by Belial's further disclosure (129-34) that an 'Armed watch' of angels is employed to supplement God's omniscience by patrolling 'the bordering Deep'. What assistance would real omniscience need?

The heavenly angels again, despite their claim on the reader's imagination, are not always paragons. More than once they are glimpsed as cosmic curiosities whose substance and properties are worth hinting at (i. 138-9, 317-18), and in one striking passage this aspect of them is boldly emphasized:

> For Spirits when they please
> Can either Sex assume, or both; so soft
> And uncompounded is thir Essence pure,
>   . . . [and] in what shape they choose
> Dilated or condens't, bright or obscure,
> Can execute thir aerie purposes,
> And works of love or enmity fulfill.   (i. 423-31)

This is unnecessarily startling ('both' in the second line is far more so than 'none' would have been), and it is not very easy to reconcile with the dignified conception of angels we had expected. Nor are the lines a necessary preparation for the shrinking of Satan's soldiers at i. 777, since that is prepared for by the simile of the bees (769-75), and adequately and tactfully explained with a single word, the 'incorporeal' of 789. Milton is not at this stage much preoccupied with the problem of angelic substance, it is true, so that his readers need not be. But the hints persist. Beelzebub discloses that the fallen angels have been *scarred* by the flames of Hell (ii. 401), and Milton speaks of their bodies' 'soft Ethereal warmth' (601). Such remarks are inoffensive but they also leave a mistrust which later passages can reawaken. In turning to these passages it is necessary to preserve an open but attentive mind.

I

God's first appearance in the poem, like Satan's, presents him at a moment when he is looking round and assessing his surroundings, though these are naturally much wider than Satan's in Hell. Perhaps his presentation is a little too declaratory at one point, when Milton baldly remarks that Heaven's angels receive from him 'Beatitude past utterance' (iii. 62). Poetry's task being to convey, not to assert, we should prefer to see this, instead of being told. Yet even so the figure is impressive, glancing from Earth to Hell with effortless circumspection, his foresight reaching out no less effortlessly into the dimension of Time (78-9). It is only when he speaks that the trouble begins.

Satan, he says, is making his adventurous journey through the cosmos in a spirit of 'rage' (80). Man, he says, 'will hark'n to his glozing lyes, And easily transgress' (93-4). Surely at once the reader's admiration hesitates, for these are half-truths only and, as such, unworthy of divinity. Satan is intrepid and determined as well as angry—a persistent current of imagery has related his journey to the voyage of an explorer—and humanity's transgression in Book Nine is something more than easy, as we shall see. Why should God withhold from devil and man such credit as is their due? The wording of his prediction 'and shall pervert' (92) is still less satisfactory, the auxiliary 'shall' (as at iv. 113 and v. 607-8) suggesting a peremptory *fiat* rather than an observation of prospective fact. In view of this suggestion his springing to his own defence ('whose fault?') and his abuse of Man as an 'ingrate' are bound to affect us rather disagreeably. The point is not that the theology which he proceeds to outline is unacceptable, still less unnecessary to the poem. It is that in representing God anthropomorphically, and then obliging him to speak his own defences at some length, Milton has conveyed a most unfortunate impression of uneasiness. The sectarian emphasis, the guilty repetitions, the whole tone of the speech is wrong. Adam and Eve cannot 'justly accuse Thir maker'; 'they themselves decreed Thir own revolt, not I'; 'they themselves ordain'd thir fall'; 'I made him . . . free to fall'; 'I formd them free'—however true such claims may be it travesties them to attribute them to a divinity already as prone as this to self-exoneration, a God who, though omnipotent, can conveniently refer to his own decree as

'Unchangeable' (127), and who promises grace to the humans merely in order that his glory shall 'excel' (133). No doubt Milton put this material into direct speech in an attempt to keep it succinct and forceful; but the effect it has is very different. God seems to be playing to the gallery of his auditors, the Son and the unfallen angels, and when 'ambrosial fragrance' fills Heaven as he falls silent we are disposed to think it little better than celestial hypocrisy. Is such a consequence justified by what has been said, still less by how it has been said?

If our first impressions of God are strangely unfavourable our first impressions of the Son are unqualifiedly approving. The contrast is hazardous. The Son's first speech is largely, if inadvertently, at his Father's expense, and it tends to confirm our incipient hostility towards God. 'O Father, gracious was that word which clos'd Thy sovran sentence', he begins, as if like us dissociating himself from God's other 'words', and he proceeds to describe the praises that will accrue to God if he is merciful. Poetic speech is to be judged by its effects, not its intentions, and here the effect is very close to tactful bribery. The Son's speech is suasive, as if he has to work on God to prevent him from changing his mind and delivering a sterner sentence, and as he speaks God's silence takes on an air of brooding petulance:

> For should Man finally be lost, should Man
> Thy creature late so lov'd, thy youngest Son
> Fall circumvented thus by fraud, though joynd
> With his own folly? that be from thee farr,
> That farr be from thee, Father. . . .   (150–4)

What troubles us is that the Son should use this tone at all. God has said 'Man . . . shall find grace' (131) and that, we feel, should be that. To urge him to a decision already taken is to suggest that he is merely volatile, that the Son must firmly remind him of his commitment, and when he speaks again we are less relieved to hear his agreement than appalled to realize that the Son should ever have seemed in doubt of it. If the Son does not know him to be absolutely just and dependable, who can? So too with the Son's concluding sentence, which contains a lurking admonition as to what will ensue if God should change his mind:

> So should thy goodness and thy greatness both
> Be questiond and blaspheam'd without defence.   (165-6)

Is it for him to risk admonishing his Father, however gently? The real difficulty is that he is obliged to state what must be God's own reasons for saving Man, but as if urging them upon his Father, to whom they might not otherwise have occurred. Two divinities cannot discuss what must be known to them both like this without at least one of them appearing fallible.

God's second speech is initially quite as unengaging as his first, and for much the same reasons. The assertion that Man will be saved through divine grace and not his own will, for example, however true, can only smack of self-aggrandizement when it is made by God himself (174-5), and this effect is recklessly emphasized by the reiteration of the eight succeeding lines: 'grace in *me* . . . *I* will renew . . . Upheld by *me* . . . By *me* upheld . . . to *me* ow All his deliv'rance, and to none but *me*' (174-82). At the same time God revives our memories of Belial's accusations by attributing irascibility to himself (186-7), an attribution we are powerless to gainsay since it recurs in both the Son's mouth (237) and his own (275) a little later. Wrath is one of the Seven Deadly Sins: ought God to be endowed with an infirmity he has forbidden to Man? The speech recovers its authority and force when he goes on to speak of his intentions for the future (188-202), but by then considerable damage has been done. Moreover, this is at once succeeded by a very awkward passage in which more self-justification is necessary, the passage turning on the proposition 'Dye hee or Justice must'. It is a ruling which any reader might be forgiven for finding arbitrary, and that is surely a sufficient reason for saying that it should never have been voiced by God. He is its author, and in his mouth it inevitably sounds like an assertion, instead of seeming a categoric law. Indeed he is made to combine the functions of legislator, judge, prosecutor, and legal apologist simultaneously, and in consequence the conditions he imposes ('unless for him Som other . . . pay The rigid satisfaction, death for death') seem very nearly bloodthirsty. Inevitably in what follows his command on our attention is gravely weakened. The Son is seen as a being so compassionate that he can adjust himself even to the abrupt and unexplained demand for a sacrifice, and once again ('thy word is past') he has to remind God of his commitment, as if in a gust of anger it might be swept aside. In view of the appearance of something like disagreement between them, and in view of his presentation of the Son as unimpeachable, Milton's subsequent attempts to make God seem impressive are much less successful than they could have been. Even the fine speech beginning 'O thou in Heav'n and Earth the only peace', which rises to the magnificently paradoxical rhetoric of 294-302, is flawed with our dubieties as to the wrath, guilt, and justice (275, 290, 294) that it premises.

First impressions, though important, are not everything, and in later passages Milton is sometimes much more successful in presenting God, and his arbitraments, than he has been in Book Three. At iv. 515-26, for example, by attributing to Satan unfair inferences about God's prohibition of the fruit of the fatal tree he very effectively discourages us from making them for ourselves. At vi. 719-20 and x. 63-5 metaphors represent God as an unclouded luminary, thus in effect conferring upon him the gentle benevolence, 'surpassing Glory', and fructifying vigour elsewhere (iii. 579-86, iv. 32-5, viii. 91-7) given to the sun. Again, the colloquy between God and Adam in Book Eight (287-499) is in some ways very appealing. Seen through the refractions of Adam's dreaming mind God is far more agreeable than when seen directly, and this continues even after Adam wakes. It is true that God is more avuncular than divine here, and that if we reflect on his demeanour its incongruity is disturbing. But if we read the lines indulgently and unreflectively their charm is undeniable: Milton's God briefly attains the benevolence of the little bearded figure in M. Jean Effel's drawings, who offers Adam a choice between a European, a Negress, a Chinese, and a Redskin, remarking that '*L'article se fournit en quatre couleurs.*' This is not God but it is disarming.

Any suggestion that Milton's occasional success with God is typical, however, would be sheer misrepresentation. As Waldock has observed, what strikes us again and again is the deliberate care he seems to have taken to ensure that a task already difficult should become impossible.[1] Artistically speaking, the God of the Old Testament is a recalcitrant enough figure in Himself, as passage after passage in the Pentateuch alone makes clear:

> And Nadab and Abihu, the sons of Aaron, took either of them his censer, and put fire therein, and put incense thereon, and offered strange fire before the Lord, which he commanded them not. And there went out fire from the Lord, and devoured them, and they died before the Lord. (Lev. 10: 1-2)
>
> And while the children of Israel were in the wilderness, they found a man that gathered sticks upon the sabbath day. . . . And the Lord said unto Moses, The man shall be surely put to death: all the congregation shall stone him with stones without the camp. And all the congregation brought him without the camp, and stoned him with stones, and he died; as the Lord commanded Moses. (Num. 15: 32-6)

Far from distracting us from accounts like these, however, as his theme really demanded, Milton habitually emphasizes the qualities and conduct they describe. One of the most obvious defects in the God of *Paradise Lost* is that he is a heterogeneous complex of ingredients, part man, part spirit, part attested biblical Presence, and part dogma. Some attempt to harmonize these qualities might have been expected from any poet of Milton's ability, but the fact is that he is often prepared to set them wantonly at odds. That he was well aware of the inscrutable dignity of such a figure common sense can assume, and many passages will show: God's wisdom is not to be comprehended by 'created mind' (iii. 705-7), God's will is Fate (vii. 173), he is omnipresent (vii. 517-18), his skirts appear 'Dark with excessive bright' (iii. 380). Yet God is also intemperately given to passion, as Satan, Gabriel, and the faithful Abdiel all attest (iv. 103-4, iv. 916, v. 890-2), and on several

---

[1] A. J. A. Waldock, *Paradise Lost and Its Critics* (Cambridge, 1947), p. 101.

occasions his speech, introduced as 'serene' or 'mild', maintains its
serenity only with an obvious effort, quickly breaking down again
into what seems to be its natural choler (viii. 317-33, viii. 368-77,
xi. 45-57). Indeed his testiness, and his readiness to impute to
others his own intemperacy, as to Adam at viii. 443 (where
Milton's use of 'dislike' for 'mislike' is perhaps revealing), makes
nonsense of his mockery of Satan for foolishly regarding him as
'transported with some fit Of Passion' (x. 626). Such a fit is, on
the face of it, all too likely. Again, he is given not only to inoffensive laughter (viii. 78) but to crude derision (ii. 191, iii. 524-5,
v. 719-32, xii. 52), he requires a Mediator before he will condes-
cend to be approached (xii. 239-40), and his speech is sometimes
grossly inappropriate, hysterically emphatic:

> I call'd and drew them thither
> My Hell-hounds, to lick up the draff and filth
> Which mans polluting Sin with taint hath shed
> On what was pure, till cramm'd and gorg'd, nigh burst
> With suckt and glutted offal . . . .   (x. 629-33)

There is a passage in Book Eight (452-8) which takes us to the
heart of these confusions, where during his colloquy with God
Adam is said to sink down 'Dazl'd and spent' after the effort of
conversing with his Maker. The reaction might be credible if at
this point God had been presented as He is in the nineteenth
chapter of Exodus, a thunderous Presence hidden in smoke and
announced by trumpets; but he is not. On the contrary he is
unexpectedly genial, so that the sudden strain on Adam seems
absurd. The fact is that, here and elsewhere in the poem, two
distinct images are being crudely superimposed: the figure of an
irritable, very occasionally friendly uncle, or stepfather, and the
figure of an awesome divinity. The human image insults the
reader's imagination whenever it becomes too clear and yet, far
from divining this, Milton is all too ready to make it clear.

> Second Omnipotence, two dayes are past,
> Two dayes, as we compute the dayes of Heav'n,

says God to his Son (vi. 684-5). Isn't this, like his self-justifications in Book Three, simply a case of 'any old mouth will do'? The point is far from trivial. Raphael is free to explain God's doctrine of Free Will (v. 524-40), Milton is free to comment on God's justice (x. 7-11), Michael is free to speak of omnipresence (xi. 335-42). But there it should have ended. When the explanations and justifications of the *De Doctrina Christiana* are intruded into God's own mouth then his 'invisible Glory' very nearly *is* transformed 'to the Image of a Brute'. No one, I believe, will contend that Milton ought to have kept God out of *Paradise Lost* entirely, as Vondel kept him out of *Lucifer:* his presence is necessary, and not just because Homer and Vergil wrote of gods. But the necessity is a very dangerous one, and it is reasonable to feel that everything possible should have been done to safeguard his presentation from miscarrying. One or other of the angels, or the poet himself, might quite well have taken over most of God's commentaries; God could have been allowed much more of mystery than he is (at x. 358-9 even Sin is given her share of it); his dwelling 'in unapproached light' *should* have been relatively unapproached; the incessant contradictions and improvisations should have been rigorously suppressed. If God is omniscient then as little as possible should be said about angels serving as his 'Eyes' (iii. 650); if he is beneficent then even the faintest suggestion of hypocrisy must be purged from what he says (vii. 150-61); if he is omnipotent then there must be no careless suggestions that his omnipotence is limited (viii. 234, ix. 927). Above all, if he is a spirit persistent analogies between Heaven and Earth should be avoided, for to emphasize them is only to draw him down to human stature, so that the reader is encouraged to judge his acts and speech by human standards, and to condemn them as vindictive and devious. Then too, if it is quite impossible to exclude such impulses to judge him, as perhaps it is, they must be kept within the narrowest bounds, and not exacerbated by palpable attempts to shade the evidence in his favour: as for example by calling his craving for self-exoneration 'pittie' (v. 220), or attributing his Son's miraculous handiwork unqualifiedly to him (iii. 708 ff.). These, one would have thought, are only the most rudimentary of precautions.

Milton takes none of them, and the neglect imposes on the reader demands that no reader should be asked to meet.

II

It can be seen that many of Milton's difficulties with God arise from his imperfectly anthropomorphic presentation. If an apparently human figure is made to speak what is literally God's truth, *knowing it is*, the effect will be priggish and distasteful and sometimes even disingenuous. Thus Theology's demand for a clearness at the outset about Man's Free Will and Poetry's demand for a characterization of God that will support our love and reverence cannot, on Milton's terms, be reconciled. The problem is complicated, however, by the presence of the Son of God, and Milton's treatment of him aggravates it. The God of the biblical story is a complex divinity, and our emotional response to Him is equally complex. Yet it is simple to this extent that, like Adam's response after the Fall (xii. 562), it fluctuates chiefly between the poles of love and fear. So long as God remains, what Adam here calls him, 'the onely God' this is more of an enrichment than a limitation. But if He is bifurcated the tendency is for our conception of Him to split in two, one half appropriating to itself His qualities of mercy, love, and gentleness, the other His qualities of severity and sternness. It is a process sometimes seen in children, who transfer upon a relative or acquaintance those qualities which disturb them in a parent. The biblical account to some extent invites such a response, for its bare essentials tend to suggest that we were made to fall by God (who does nothing to hinder Satan's attack on Man) and then redeemed by His Son.

This invitation to divide the concept of God *Paradise Lost* not only accepts, but seems to accept with enthusiasm. Our first view of Heaven reveals the Son as the merciful complement of his Father's resentful rigour, the only volunteer on Man's behalf and counsel for Man's defence, and after this introduction the occasionally precative tone of his speech is most ill-judged:

> Thou at the sight
> Pleas'd, out of Heaven shalt look down and smile . . .
> [And I shall] see thy face, wherein no cloud
> Of anger shall remain, but peace assur'd,
> And reconcilement; wrauth shall be no more
> Thenceforth, but in thy presence Joy entire.   (iii. 256-65)

Lines like these have a quality almost of pathos, the pathos of utter devotion to an unworthy superior. God appears as a cruel tyrant whose equanimity can only be restored by the sacrifice of those who love him best. Once this impression is fixed (and when the angels give nearly twenty more lines of praise to the Son than to him it hardens perceptibly) the reader's approach to the poem is adjusted to comply with it and fixed in turn. In what relates to God he begins to read like a book-reviewer: conceding as little as possible, deliberately misunderstanding in order to disagree, querying propositions which in their context are unexceptionable. We find ourselves agreeing with Satan that gratitude to such a figure is 'burthensome' (iv. 53); we refuse to give God credit for his Grace or his delight in Man (vii. 571, xi. 23); and Adam's supposition that he can be wearied by the 'assiduous cries' of his creatures (xi. 310) strikes us as a plausible criticism. Any negligence in the presentation of the Father—and it is not to seek—is interpreted against him. 'Who can extenuate thee?' becomes, in fact, an irritated watchword.

On the other hand the Son, often because of this, can virtually do no wrong. Let him be 'full of wrauth' (vi. 826): it is merely a case of 'whom thou hat'st, I hate' (vi. 734), a further evidence of his dutiful obedience. Let him inflict Homeric 'Plagues' (vi. 838): the violence is vicarious, and if any blame attaches to it the blame is God's. When after the Fall he says to Adam

> Hast thou eaten of the Tree
> Whereof I gave thee charge thou shouldst not eat? (x. 122-3)

we do not inwardly chide him for asking a question to which he knows the answer, but presume at once that he is trying to make things easier for Adam, by leaving room for confession and repentance. When the syntax of his speech is ambiguous, exposing him to a charge of egotism, we instinctively ignore the ambiguity:

> thou always seekst
> To glorifie thy Son, I alwayes thee,
> As is most just.   (vi. 724-6)

Our attitude is not merely a negative matter of abstentions and refusals. It is positive because the Son's virtues are positive, and positively shown, in the tone of his minor speeches (v. 719-37) as much as in his major actions. He is 'By Merit more then Birthright Son of God' (iii. 309) and his merits are continually apparent. He pleads on Man's behalf and undertakes to save us; he drives the devils from Heaven; he creates our universe with (literally) an easy flick of the wrist. All the glory of that Creation, all the potency Book Seven implies, accrues to him, not to his Father, because it is the Son whom we see creating before our eyes. Moreover our faint suspicion that what the Son creates, God in effect later destroys, is never wholly expunged, and we are free to interpret the proposition 'to create Is greater then created to destroy' (vii. 606-7) in an unintended and unsympathetic way.

Milton's treatment of the Son is not absolutely flawless. At times the language applied to him is poetically inadequate, as in the reference to his 'conspicuous count'nance' at iii. 385, or nonsensical, as in the lines

> Son in whose face invisible is beheld
> Visibly, what by Deitie I am.   (vi. 681-2)[1]

At times what is said of him is rather contradictory: though 'unwearied' by his creation at vii. 552, for instance, he is found 'resting' with his Father (the word is even repeated) at 592-3, when it is finished. Then too at times our loyal regard for him is subjected to fleeting but unnecessary strain, as when he seems about to impose a mild sentence on Adam and Eve because he knows

---

[1] In his *Critical Observations on Shakespeare* (2nd edn., London, 1748, p. 202) John Upton conjectured that *invisible* should be '*th*' *invisible*: TO ΑΟΡΑΤΟΝ', and his conjecture was approved by Todd. The emendation gives better sense, if poorer syntax, but today only Professor B. A. Wright still accepts it.

that it will one day also fall upon himself (x. 71-7). But these are trivial uncertainties nda quite inadequate to restore the balance between God and himself in our regard. It is something of a puzzle to see why an Arian like Milton should have given such dignity and refinement, in comparison with his Father, to the figure of the Son. A fanciful commentator might draw attention to the passage in Book Ten (1060-85) where Adam predicts that God will instruct the human pair in the use of fire, thus enabling them to endure the cold of winter. Adam's own words show that he is referring to the Son, the divinity who lately clothed Eve and himself, and it is tempting to see a parallel with the myth of the rebellious fire-giver, friend to Man and foe to God. Common sense will remind us, however, that even if a parallel with Prometheus could be upheld at his point it would be merely local, a symptom rather than a cause, and thus inadequate to explain the treatment of the Son elsewhere. I think the real key to the Son's portrayal lies in the doctrine of the Incarnation, but as this point will come up more appropriately later it need not be considered here.

III

Milton's difficulties in presenting God are sometimes represented as insurmountable, but most of them could have been avoided if he had used the angels more effectively. As has been noted, the chief tension within the God of *Paradise Lost* exists between his majesty, which should be inaccessible and mysterious, and other less ineffable qualities: his anger, or the geniality seen in his colloquy with Adam in Book Eight. Properly handled, the angels might have removed this tension: they could have taken over God's practical functions and left his majesty unqualified and intact. If it is necessary to explain Free Will at length, as indeed it is, the explanation is best left to Raphael. If it is advisable to show God's friendliness to Adam before the Fall, as again perhaps it is, an angel, Heaven's delegate, is a better instrument for the purpose than God himself, reduced and circumscribed, can ever be. Vondel

seems to have grasped the point instinctively, and in all his plays
(even the early *Het Pascha*, where the Deity is a 'voice off') he
proceeds with such skill that there is never any call for God to take
the stage himself. In *Paradise Lost* such an exclusion would have
been difficult, and perhaps unwise, but God's appearances could
have been much more exalted and illustrious than they are.

It is not only the angels' function that is mishandled. The poet's
whole concept of them seems inappropriate and refractory. At the
root of this refractoriness lies Milton's doctrine of the materiality
of all Creation, a doctrine quite acceptably set forth by Raphael
and at this date sufficiently familiar to students of the poem.
Unlike the Gnostics, who held that matter was essentially evil,
Milton believed that matter and spirit differed only in degree, not
kind, and that each contained the potentiality for goodness,
though in their different degrees:

> O *Adam*, one Almightie is, from whom
> All things proceed, and up to him return,
> If not deprav'd from good, created all
> Such to perfection, one first matter all,
> Indu'd with various forms, various degrees
> Of substance, and in things that live, of life; &c. (v. 469-90)

But doctrines acceptable in theory are easy to abuse in practice,
and when this belief is applied directly to the angels the abuse is
blatant. For poet and reader alike it is again chiefly a matter of
indecision, of not knowing on what plane the poem's characters
exist. On one plane, the plane on which acquaintance with their
defeated opponents inclines us to take them, the angels are superb.
They are 'Celestial Ardors' (v. 249), flames of zeal (v. 807), their
swiftness in flight is amazing (viii. 110-14), they are more impressive than the planets (vi. 310-15), they outshine the moon as
gold does silver (iv. 554, 609, 798), they are 'Thrones, Domina-
tions, Princedoms, Vertues, Powers' (v. 601). This is as it should
be. What troubles us is the poet's tendency to treat their figurative
titles literally, to bring them down to earth. Consider the lines
describing Raphael's arrival in Paradise:

> . . . To all the Fowles he seems
> A *Phœnix*, gaz'd by all, as that sole Bird
> When to enshrine his reliques in the Sun's
> Bright Temple, to *Ægyptian Theb's* he flies.
> At once on th'Eastern cliff of Paradise
> He lights, and to his proper shape returns
> A Seraph wingd. (v. 271-7)

Raphael is not, despite 'seems', merely likened to a phoenix in an effective metaphor. He is actually disguised as one, a disclosure which is much less effective and which sets one wondering what the purpose of the disguise can be. So too the fine phrase 'Celestial Ardors', when Milton comes to enlarge on it, seems to be largely a matter of digestion, related to the 'concoctive heate' with which, like incinerators, the angels sublimate their solid food (v. 433-43).

Here, of course, the angels find their other level, such as it is, a level on which their materiality proves to be quite incorrigible. What is most striking about the relevant passages in Book Five is simply their utter lack of tact. It is tactless to apply words like 'digest' and 'assimilate' to angels (v. 412), if only because they raise an involuntary thought of angelic excretion, which must then also be accounted for (438-9). It is tactless, after describing the 'real hunger' angels feel (437), to introduce the notion of angelic lust (448-9), even if only to deny it, especially if their capacity to love is later to be blushingly admitted (viii. 618). It is tactless, even if only by implication, to defend the angels against a charge of gluttony (v. 451-2), and it is still more tactless to intrude an explicit defence against this charge in the second edition of the poem (637-41), whatever editors may mumble of an 'inspired addition to the text'. Inevitably our responses are conditioned and cramped after such passages as these, and once again we find ourselves reading with an attention that has become niggling and mistrustful. If Milton wants his angels viewed as curiosities we shall observe his wishes, keeping ourselves alert to all their more ridiculous attributes.

Angelic behaviour being frequently imperfect, there is much in the poem on which this intolerance can fasten. Uriel seems to disapprove of laziness in angels (iii. 700-1), yet he himself slides down the sunbeams like a lazy child instead of flying (iv. 589-92). On at least three occasions (vi. 19-20, vi. 547, x. 227-8) angels are made to announce what is already known to their hearers, which makes them seem futile. They are said to walk the earth in their unseen millions (iv. 677-8), a statement which everything else in the poem leads us to disbelieve. And their conduct at the time of the building of the Tower of Babel, whatever Milton's Homeric and biblical precedents, seems infantile and undignified, like peasants giggling and elbowing at a peepshow:

> Great laughter was in Heav'n
> And looking down.   (xii. 59-60)

I put these criticisms bluntly because it seems perfectly fair to do so: Milton's whole treatment of the angels encourages us to be blunt. In the exordium to Book Nine he remarks that 'Impreses quaint, Caparisons and Steeds' are not enough to make a hero, that a character is judged by what he is and does and not by his appearance, but applied to his own angels this form of judgement proves awkwardly testing. The mass of angels are seldom engaged in anything more impressive than a song and dance—Milton's earnest assurance that their harps are never out of tune (iii. 366), for all these instruments' acknowledged instability, tends to make them not more but less impressive—and when Satan dubs them 'the Ministrelsie of Heav'n' and decries their servility (vi. 168-9) his words seem all too apt. Nor are the angels' defects defects in them alone: inevitably they disturb our attitude to the incidents in the poem. The ending of Book Four is a case in point. Here we see Satan and Gabriel face to face, two angry controversialists, and a group of heavenly angels whose spears an inappropriately debilitating simile has likened to swaying ears of harvest wheat (iv. 979-85). Milton huffs and puffs, telling us of 'dreadful deeds' and 'violence' to come, but our scepticism has been roused too far. We cannot believe that any real violence will follow when on one side there is merely a group of minstrels armed with toy spears—men, as it were, of straw—and when God intervenes to avert disaster it seems the act of a busybody or a poltroon. In view of Gabriel's assurance that Satan is 'Not likely to part hence without contest' (872), and the tremendous power previously attributed to the devil, it is even possible, just here, to feel that God knows Satan will prevail, and that his method of avoiding a defeat, even a minor defeat, is underhand and unfair.

IV

Individual angels fare rather better than the category in general, though not much. Occasionally their weakness is due to plain inconsistency, as when Uriel, 'held The sharpest sighted Spirit of all in Heav'n' (iii. 691), unaccountably loses sight of Satan's movements on the earth (iv. 572-3), or when a 'genial Angel' is said to bring the newly created Eve to Adam (iv. 708-13), an action later attributed, of course, to God himself (viii. 485).[1] But usually the inconsistencies are less obtrusive, the evidence against a particular angel gathering almost imperceptibly, at a preconscious rather than a conscious level. When we stop for a moment to consider we are often surprised to find how unfavourable our attitude has become.

Consider the case of Gabriel, an angel of whom we see comparatively little. He is at first well characterized as a mighty warrior, 'Chief of th' Angelic Guards', and his speech has just the right touch of military succinctness and decision:

> But if within the circuit of these walks,
> In whatsoever shape he lurk, of whom
> Thou tellst, by morrow dawning I shall know. (iv. 586-8)

No fool, he realizes at once that Satan wishes to strike at Adam and Eve, and he briefs his angels accordingly:

---

[1] The discrepancy may reflect the two senses that can be given to the Hebrew phrase *mal'ak Jahweh:* 'angel of Jahweh' or 'special visitation of Jahweh'. But it is unexplained and therefore perplexing. So too in Book Twelve, though God is said to be represented by an angel (201), he also seems to be present in person (208-10).

Leave unsearcht no nook,
But chiefly where those two fair Creatures Lodge,
Now laid perhaps asleep secure of harme.   (789-91)

Yet when Satan is found, and he confronts him, his brisk and
soldierly manner disappears. Satan is described as speaking 'in
scorn' (902), which seems from what he says to be a slight distortion, but the statement that Gabriel replies 'Disdainfully half
smiling', with its suggestion of supercilious vanity, agrees closely
with the words of his reply. As soon as he speaks it is obvious that
Satan's questioning of his wisdom has stung him, and his response
is to throw doubts on Satan's wisdom in return. His egotism,
just here, seems very nearly as touchy as Satan's; and unlike
Zephon's, which was grim (855), his irony is jeering. Indeed the
tone of his speech is not very different from Satan's at iv. 375-87,
where derisive irony also figures. Perhaps the pique and abusive-
ness of Milton's prose pamphlets has crept into both passages;
in any case what is natural in Satan appears most unnatural in an
angel as valiant and august as Gabriel. The speech really needs to
be read in context for these effects to be properly felt, but even an
extract will suggest some of the uncertainty in its phrasing:

The warlike Angel mov'd,
Disdainfully half smiling thus repli'd.
O loss of one in Heav'n to judge of wise,
Since *Satan* fell, whom follie overthrew,
And now returns him from his prison scap't,
Gravely in doubt whether to hold them wise
Or not, who ask what boldness brought him hither
Unlicenc't from his bounds in Hell prescrib'd;
So wise he judges it to fly from pain
However, and to scape his punishment. &c.   (902 ff.)

Like Abdiel's or Michael's in Book Six, Gabriel's taunts are out
of character, nor does it make them any less unsuitable to compare
the κερτομίαι of Homeric champions: these are *angels*. What
farther weakens his presentation is the forensic style of argument
he is given, petty and pompous, the quibbling over words like

'wise', 'pain', and 'faithful'. One cannot believe that a 'Celestial Ardor' would speak like this, nor even that a 'warriour Angel' would.

Raphael's case is similar, and we see and hear far more of him in the poem. On the face of it his characterization seems to be agreeable: he is impressively if perhaps rather concretely described (v. 277-85), he is 'affable' (vii. 41) and 'sociably mild' (xi. 234), and even his voice is pleasant (vii. 68). Yet his good qualities become less absolute than at first sight they seem. For one thing he is not above punning, just after Satan has been doing so (vi. 558 ff., 578), which makes him seem eager to emulate the devil. For another his gift for prophecy strikes one as dubious, the 'prescience' of a character in a novel like *Ivanhoe* predicting firearms (vi. 501-6). For yet another his affability, though much is made of it, is after all enjoined. God has commanded him to converse with Adam 'as friend with friend' (v. 229) so that Milton's many references to his genial manner seem strangely indulgent, like praising a sergeant for standing at ease when his commanding officer has given the order. Raphael admits that he is under orders in a speech which, like Gabriel's in Book Four, is somehow off the pitch we should expect from him:

> Yet what thou canst attain, which best may serve
> To glorifie the Maker, and inferr
> Thee also happier, shall not be withheld
> Thy hearing, such Commission from above
> I have receav'd, to answer thy desire
> Of knowledge within bounds; beyond abstain
> To ask, nor let thine own inventions hope
> Things not reveal'd . . . . (vii. 115-22)

What troubles us is the discrepancy between his alleged affability and the stuffy tones of his speech, now patronizing, now preaching. He seems excessively concerned to stress the limitations of Adam's nature (see also v. 503-5 and vii. 640), so that a word like 'condescention' applied to him takes on an unintended flavour of distaste (viii. 9, 649); and he is given to moralizing admonitions which, though sound enough, are something less than affable

(vii. 512-13, viii. 561 ff.). Again, that is, the principle of 'any old mouth will do' appears to be at work. No one will claim that Raphael is as unsatisfactory as God. At times his friendliness is obvious and engaging, as in the compliments he pays to Adam at viii. 218-28. But the flaws in his presentation allow some of his Master's colours to rub off on him, and make it hard to accept him without hesitation. Sometimes he appears quite unconscious of his auditor, thoughtlessly flattering Adam (vii. 505-11) and then telling him of things he already knew (vii. 561). Sometimes we suspect him of 'editing' his tale so as to make it more admonitory. Two lines that he says the angels sang, for instance, are inappropriate to the occasion he is describing and are pretty clearly an insertion of his own (vii. 631-2). Sometimes he is scarcely even lucid, as in what he has to say about the cosmos in Book Eight. Here he is all too human—conjecturing, going back on his conjectures, and then throwing up the subject with a moral rider to hide his bewilderment and ineffectuality:

> Sollicit not thy thoughts with matters hid.   (viii. 167)

A fair comment would be that he has himself been soliciting Adam's thoughts on the subject for upwards of fifty involved lines. Again, though he carries out his orders sufficiently to warn Adam that Satan 'now is plotting how he may seduce Thee also from obedience' (vi. 901-2), he never mentions the devil's propinquity, so that it is hard to see how Adam later knows that Satan is 'somwhere nigh at hand' (ix. 256).

It will perhaps be said, justly, that many of these points are trivial in themselves. That does not mean that their cumulative effect can be ignored, especially in a poem as closely wrought as this. When the ruler of Heaven is as unprepossessing as Milton's God his servants are not exempt from a certain suspicion, and this even occasional lapses in their presentation will tend to confirm. Angels are likely to be appraised strictly on their merits, which must therefore be consistently angelic. The point is, not that Gabriel or Raphael is unpleasant, but that Milton's estimate of them, as of their Ruler, is perceptibly higher than any estimate which a reader is allowed to form: in what pertains to them he is haunted by the discrepancy between his own reactions and the poet's. This is what makes Michael comparatively easy to accept, for on the whole his presentation is much more integrated and coherent, especially as he appears in Books Eleven and Twelve. By having him repeat God's words of instruction to him (xi. 97-8, 261-2) Milton makes it quite clear that he is carrying out orders, and no attempt is made to set his actions to his own personal credit. Thus he has a claim on us simply because no specious claims are made on his behalf. Moreover he carries out God's orders implicitly and thoroughly, both the letter and the spirit. His demeanour is just what it should be (xi. 249-50) and his tone is exactly right: terse, non-committal, but devoid of all hostility (xi. 251-62). These are first impressions in a sense, despite his brief appearances earlier in the poem, and they do much to break down any prejudices that might be forming against him. We forget the passing deflation he suffered at vi. 45, when the un-impressive Gabriel was placed next in military prowess to him, and we are ready to overlook the misogynism apparently attributed to him by Adam at xi. 236-7: 'whom not to offend, With reverence I must meet, and [Eve] retire.' Later we find that Michael is even milder than God's instructions have obliged him to be. He speaks gently to Eve (xi. 286-92), he raises the swooning Adam with a compassionate hand (xi. 421-2), and like Adam he is 'mov'd' at the sight of Cain's fratricide (xi. 453). Such actions are enough to confirm our regard for him and, once established, it continues more or less intact until the end. It is true that his recommendation of temperance (xi. 530 ff.) is somewhat un-convincing, in view of the grim old age to which he says it will lead, and that his remark to Adam, 'I see him, but thou canst not' (xii. 128), sounds unfairly patronizing, since Adam's inability to see Abraham is due entirely to him (xii. 11). It is also true that the sectarian bias in some of his lines (xii. 507 ff.) seems out of place. But unlike Raphael's these lapses strike us as minor matters, and it is interesting to inquire why they should. No doubt it is partly because our sympathetic attention has already been given, so that a major lapse is needed before it can be reasonably withdrawn. It is by what they say and do that the individual angels are judged, and from the moment of his arrival in Paradise Michael has behaved and spoken with unusual authority. Still, I feel that another reason why we sympathize with him is because Milton himself did so: more fully, that is, than he could sympathize with Gabriel or Raphael, or even God. It is interesting to notice that in the last two books Michael has the appearance, not of an angel, but of a man (xi. 239-40). And it is still more interesting to notice that his human appearance—necessarily inferior, one would have thought, to the appearance of angels—strikes Adam as more princely than that of the other angels he has seen (xi. 296-8). Something comparable to the indulgence with which the Son of God is seen is surely at work in the case of this near-human figure too. Certainly the Son's status in our eyes is unrivalled by any other inhabitant of Heaven. But Michael, at any rate in the concluding books, attains a status which, though inferior, is not altogether different. The other heavenly personages, especially God, exist on a much lower level. Creative sympathy seems relatively withdrawn from them, and they function more in the manner of marionettes, externally manipulated, seen from outside.

Chapter Three

SATAN AND HIS ANGELS

I

OUR introduction to the fallen angels in Book One is made first, and appropriately, through their leader. Much has been written about this early section of the poem, but I do not know that any commentator has pointed out how inauspiciously it begins. Our very first glimpse of Satan as a character, the first action he performs, is phrased in such a way as to invite a reader's hesitation.

> Round he throws his baleful eyes
> That witness'd huge affliction and dismay
> Mixt with obdurate pride and stedfast hate.   (i. 56-8)

In which of its two senses is 'witness'd to be accepted here? Both seem unnatural. If the word means 'bore witness to' or 'revealed' (its older sense) the lines presuppose extraordinarily expressive eyes, capable of projecting almost any combination of 'huge' emotions. In view of the darkness—which, if 'visible' (63), is also 'utter' (72)—there even seems to be some suggestion (cf. 'sparkling blaz'd', line 194) that they are phosphorescent. If on the other hand 'witness'd' means 'saw', how could recumbent forms 'Thick as Autumnal Leaves' contrive to express 'dismay' or 'pride', particularly again when all is dark? Are Satan's eyes like fireworks, or a cat's?

Even less satisfactory is the scene as a whole, the tableau that is presented. The devils are discovered 'rowling in the fiery Gulfe' (52), 'o'rewhelm'd With Floods and Whirlwinds of tempestuous fire' (77), 'weltring' (78) in 'a fiery Deluge' (68) where the molten brimstone is boiling and tossing (i. 184, ii. 183). Yet despite the

violent disturbance on all sides there is apparently 'silence' (i. 83),
and despite the agony they are suffering—the 'pain of un-
extinguishable fire', as Moloch later calls it (ii. 88)—they converse
in sentences of Ciceronian elaboration:

> . . . yet not for these,
> Nor what the Potent Victor in his rage
> Can else inflict, do I repent or change,
> Though chang'd in outward lustre, that fixt mind
> And high disdain, from sence of injur'd merit,
> That with the mightiest rais'd me to contend,
> And to the fierce contention brought along
> Innumerable force of Spirits arm'd
> That durst dislike his reign, and me preferring,
> His utmost power with adverse power oppos'd
> In dubious Battel on the Plains of Heav'n,
> And shook his throne.   (i. 94-105)

Thus Satan, in the first speech of the epic. Surely as little as
possible should hinder the reader's acceptance of its convention-
ality, and surely his knowledge that the speaker is immersed in a
surf of liquid fire is enough to make it ludicrous. The accents are
vehement, but no more tortured than those of a man relaxing in
a turkish bath: in fact it is some such picture that Milton's
description of Satan 'With Head up-lift above the wave' suggests
(193). To argue that his equanimity at this point is the measure of
Satan's fortitude would be to seize on the most implausible of
excuses for the passage, and to do them justice Milton's warmest
advocates make no such claim. 'The entire speech', says Professor
Hanford, 'is made disjointed to indicate Satan's emotional stress.'[1]
That is indeed what the situation demands, but is it even remotely
true? Satan's pain is intense (54-6, 125), a fitting punishment for
his transgressions, and Milton means us to accept it as intense. No
doubt he means us to see as well that Satan is still undaunted, still
capable of voicing his defiance through gritted teeth, while the
boiling fire slaps at his face. But the self-possession that these

---

[1] *The Poems of John Milton*, ed. James Holly Hanford (2nd edn., New York,
1953), p. 208 n.

oratorical periods convey is wholly out of place, and feebly incongruous.

What is at work here might be called the fallacy of eating cake and having it too, and it involves a conflation of effects not unlike the conflation found in the figure of God, the superimposition of conflicting appearances within a single frame. On the one hand Hell has to be a terrifying prison, fiery and turbulent; on the other Satan's first speech must ring imperiously and boldly if it is to sound the keynote of his scale. Neither requirement offers much difficulty in itself, but when they are carelessly associated they contradict each other: Satan's composure makes the flames of Hell seem tepid, while the flames make his composure seem absurd. The fallacy lies in hunting for an immediate effect at each point as it offers without sufficiently considering how they are likely to consort together. It is a practice that has been observed and justly condemned in the plays of Beaumont and Fletcher,[1] yet Milton is much given to it in *Paradise Lost* and his indiscretions seem to have been largely overlooked. Another case is the line which precedes Satan's first speech, where we are told that in Hell 'hope never comes' (66). To be effective this has to be categorical, and being categorical it is contradicted when Satan's followers are later described as being 'somwhat rais'd By false presumptuous hope' (ii. 521-2) or by 'Fallacious hope' (ii. 568)—to say nothing of Moloch's and Mammon's patently hopeful speeches during the Great Consult. Again, at various points in Books One and Two we are persuaded to visualize the chains which bind the devils on the lake of fire (i. 210; ii. 169, 183, 196), yet when Satan rises from it they offer absolutely no resistance and seem to be purely meta-phorical (i. 221 ff.). Two of the most flagrant instances of artistic op-portunism or effect-hunting come later, again in connexion with Satan. When he confronts 'the grieslie terrour' of Death his ability to stand 'Unterrifi'd' is clearly intended to impress us (ii. 708), and when he roosts like a cormorant in the Tree of Life we are expected to relish the irony of his nescience regarding its fruit:

---

[1] See L. C. Knights, *Drama and Society in the Age of Jonson* (London, 1937), pp. 294-7; U. M. Ellis-Fermor, *The Jacobean Drama* (London, 1936), chapter xi.

> Nor on the vertue thought
> Of that life-giving Plant, but only us'd
> For prospect, what well us'd had bin the pledge
> Of immortality.   (iv. 198-201)

On both occasions Satan is assumed to be a mortal spirit, so that
Milton can dramatize his behaviour, but seemingly without
regard to other passages with which this view conflicts. Moloch
may be in doubt about the fallen angels' immortality (ii. 99), but
wiser heads like Satan (i. 116-17, 318, 622) and Beelzebub (138-9)
know that they are immortal, while Belial doubts whether
Omnipotence Itself could ever destroy them (ii. 151-4). Even the
poet admits that they are 'Spirits immortal' (i. 53, ii. 553). In each
of these cases—and the list is far from exhaustive—cake is eaten
and yet presumed to be undiminished, coherence yielding to the
challenge of particular dramatic opportunities yet being still relied
on as coherence. The picture of an angelic orator wallowing in
fiery turbulence is not so starkly irregular but it is much less
forceful than it could have been.

   A poor beginning, however, need not obscure the subtlety with
which Book One proceeds. Part of the poet's skill is applied to
unfolding the plot of the poem: the devils' new approach through
guile is deftly, that is to say casually, introduced (121), and the
reader is made aware too of the irony of their attempt to pervert
God's ends to their own advantage (162-5, 210 ff.). Even more
skill goes into the presentation of the characters, particularly the
presentation of Satan. His lies are made to ring with conviction,
and by permitting him to address them to the reader rather than
Beelzebub (who, for example, would know all too well that nine
days before God had not 'Doubted his Empire' under their
threatening) Milton endows them with all the clarity and vigour
that they need. Indeed what ought to awaken doubts as to Satan's
veracity, even more than an occasional phrase like 'Vaunting
aloud' (126), is this same clarity. Real truth is seldom as simple as
he would make it, nor does honesty lend itself so readily to slogans,
as can be seen by comparing Abdiel's 'Reign thou in Hell thy
Kingdom, let mee serve In Heav'n God ever blest' (vi. 183-4) with

his much more emphatic 'Better to reign in Hell, then serve in Heav'n' (i. 263). What we are listening to is only one side of an argument, and simply because there are no interruptions it can be made to sound firm and coherent. Milton justifiably expects our listening to be done with some scepticism. Satan may seem to welcome his new domain (250-2), but he lets slip the phrase 'unhappy Mansion' (268), which should prepare us for the way his mind will leap forward from Hell at ii. 434, already thinking of it as a 'convex', from outside, and even for his denunciation of it much later, when he can leave it, as 'this infernal Pit Abominable, accurst, the house of woe' (x. 464-5). He may rant of freedom (259) but we must be prepared to learn from Gabriel that he 'Once fawn'd, and cring'd, and servilly ador'd Heav'ns awful Monarch' (iv. 959-60). His claims to steadfastness of mind (253), to having warred with God himself (623-4), to having 'emptied' Heaven (633) will all be disproved later, and that they are should come as no surprise. Nevertheless our reservations must not be allowed to harden into a disbelief as simple and complete as his own assertiveness. What is needed, and what Milton's presentation normally ensures from all but diabolist or Christian apologists, is an attention like Keats's 'negative capability':[1] an attention which will accept the evidence as it comes, whatever its inner tensions and ambivalences, and which will then possess it in suspension, without straining at it to prove that Satan is either a hero or a fool. The figure that confronts us is a living one, with all the complexity consequent on life. It is, moreover, a highly paradoxical figure when seen through human eyes, for, however outrageous its depravities, it is immeasurably superior to any human figure we have ever seen or ever could see. Satan has authority. When Beelzebub seems irresolute, the yes-man torn between his discretion and his sense (like Belial's later) that their cause is lost, his leader quickly pulls him up (156). When their followers are swarming to the shore a flourish of Satan's spear brings order out of the chaos almost as effectively as the Son later does with his

---

[1] Letter to George and Thomas Keats, 22 December, 1817. See *The Letters of John Keats*, ed. Maurice Buxton Forman (4th edn., O.U.P., 1952), p. 71.

golden compasses (347-58). Satan is force apotheosized. Though he is not directly compared to Etna the passage about the volcano is sufficiently involved to leave the reader with a dazzled impression of his violence and power (230-7). These qualities are as prodigious as his appearance but they are not allowed to mask the other qualities that he also has, and simultaneously. Recklessness is one. So uncontrollable is his hostility to Heaven that he will prosecute it whether the outcome be in conquest or destruction, telling Beelzebub that their aim must be 'to try what may be yet Regaind in Heav'n, or what more lost in Hell' (269-70). Blindness is another, or perhaps it is less like blindness than like the psychopath's habit of shutting himself off from reality in a more comfortable world of his own creating. He still refers to his army as 'the Host of Heav'n', not Hell (635), and he persuades himself and his followers that merely by challenging God they have accomplished something, regardless of the fact of their defeat (638). All through Book One there are unpleasant or ambiguous touches to disturb and render fluid the dominant impression of his commanding strength. He is like Leviathan but he is also treacherous, a seeming island liable to submerge (200-8). His shield is like the moon seen through a telescope, but the moon's face is 'spotty' (291), a word suggesting blemishes or disease. His apostrophes to his troops begin impressively, but on occasion their resonant defiance tails off very effectively in regret:

> O Myriads of immortal Spirits, O Powers
> Matchless, but with th' Almighty, and that strife
> Was not inglorious, though th' event was dire,
> As this place testifies, and this dire change
> Hateful to utter.   (622-6)

Again, to discourage the reader still farther from simplifying what is before him Milton very skilfully reverses this technique, allowing ostensibly limiting descriptions to serve as enhancements. Consider the references to Satan's pride. At first they are almost as derogatory as one would expect (527, 572), but the word has also been used in a neutral sense (533) and it twists and expands with

every reappearance until it seems to represent a virtue: Satan
stands 'proudly eminent' above his army (590), watching them
from under brows 'Of dauntless courage, and considerate Pride'
(603). Consider in this same passage the description of his
features:

> Dark'n'd so, yet shon
> Above them all th' Arch Angel: but his face
> Deep scars of Thunder had intrencht, and care
> Sat on his faded cheek . . . .   (599-602)

His scars, like his faded cheek, are here adduced as impairments of
his brightness, but the nominal sense is surely an illusion. We
accept them as the insignia of his rank, the trophies won by
honour in the War, and when immediately we come to 'cruel
his eye' we do not think of cruelty so much as ruthlessness, or even
plain determination. The poet's aim is obviously to play on our
irresolution, to hold us in suspense, and he is wonderfully successful. The equivocality of Satan's appearance, speech, and conduct
is partly accounted for by the fact that his identity is in a state of
transition, like an ember plucked from the fire and slowly fading
(591-2). But it is also functional, to arrest and hold attention. If we
reduce these vivid colours to common black or white we only
show ourselves unequal to the poetry.

In what relates to the devils Milton is almost equally adroit,
though this adroitness too is often missed. It is not enough, for
instance, to approve the 'catalogue of heroes' (381-505) merely
for its resemblance to the similar catalogue in Book Two of the
Iliad. One must look farther, appreciating the deftness of the
introductions it effects and, even more, the subtle and continuous
allusions it provides to Milton's subject. The suggestiveness of its
details is astonishing. Moloch misleads Solomon as his commander
is to mislead Eve; the pleasant valley of Hinnom, like Eden,
becomes a 'Type of Hell'; Josiah drives the Baalim down to Hell
as, later in the poem, the Son of God will drive the devils;
Solomon is 'Beguil'd by fair Idolatresses' just as Adam will be
by Eve; the 'wanton passions' of Sion's daughters recall the lusts

of Satan and Sin, as also of Adam and Eve after the Fall; Dagon the 'Sea Monster' casts us back to 'that Sea-beast *Leviathan*', and his deformity is very like Sin's; the 'wandring Gods disguis'd in brutish forms' might be a direct reference to Satan disguised as the serpent; and so on and on. Less remote than these connexions are the links between the devils and their leader, and here too Milton supplies a richness of interest which should not be overlooked. That once or twice his presentation wavers—that it is awkward, for instance, to say that the devils are superior to the Titans (576-9) when some have previously been identified with them (508-12)— may be conceded without embarrassment. Such a slip is trivial in comparison with his success, the skill with which the devils are made to blazon Satan's qualities abroad, at the same time reflecting back upon their leader a richer and more revealing light than he might otherwise have stood in. Thus a speech of Beelzebub's in which he attributes the army's bewilderment merely to their headlong fall through space (272-82) reminds us of Satan's own capacity for self-delusion. Again, when Satan has suggested a new approach less hazardous than open war the devils are shown behaving defiantly and fiercely (663-9), a reaction which promptly raises doubts about their valour, and their leader's too. The very trumpet that announces their orders (754) we shall later find to be an imitation of 'the loud Ethereal Trumpet' that gives commands in Heaven (vi. 60), thus suggesting another trait of Satan soon to be evident: his mimicry of God. Above all we notice how, like Satan himself, the devils seem to shift and alter, hovering between the poles of horror and magnificence, grandeur and menace.

As if to underline its importance this is made to appear at once, in the first substantial description Milton gives of them. They are

> A multitude, like which the populous North
> Pour'd never from her frozen loyns, to pass
> *Rhene* or the *Danaw*, when her barbarous Sons
> Came like a Deluge on the South, and spread
> Beneath *Gibralter* to the *Lybian* sands.
> Forthwith from every Squadron and each Band
> The Heads and Leaders thither hast where stood

Thir great Commander; Godlike shapes and forms
Excelling human, Princely Dignities
And Powers that earst in Heaven sat on Thrones.   (351-60)

The passage presents the same kind of vitality, on a diffuse scale, that an oxymoron has succinctly. It is perhaps no accident that the condensed figure appears repeatedly in the early books of *Paradise Lost:* 'darkness visible', 'Arch Angel ruind', 'precious bane', 'bad eminence', 'Black fire', 'Burns frore'. Such collocations take their life from the tension between syntax and meaning. So far as meaning goes words like 'visible', 'ruind', 'precious', &c., tend naturally to fly off from the nouns and verbs they are made to modify, but syntax restrains them, tethering them in place. The effect is that a sort of vibrancy is set up within the phrase, not unlike that of the armature in an electric buzzer, a restlessness and vigour of language unobtainable in any other way. Though its energy is lower this same vibrancy is present in the passage quoted, for the reader's mind must struggle to reconcile the view of the devils as a predatory host of barbarians (or, in the lines preceding, an even more predatory swarm of locusts) with their 'Godlike shapes and forms' and 'Princely Dignities'. The impossibility of ever doing this completely and finally leaves the verse with a special forcefulness, imparting to the devils themselves a striking and enigmatic fascination.

Broadly speaking, the impression left by Satan's army is one of hugeness and menace. Their brightness, like that of the meteor to which their ensign is compared (537) or of the comet that Satan resembles (ii. 708), is portentous, threatening. Their violent shout (i. 542) has nothing in common with the dulcet shout of jubilee heard in Heaven (iii. 345-9), and after it their silent movements are positively frightening, betokening as they do a formidable pitch of discipline. Because their constancy in a lost cause might appear foolish Milton allows us to see it only through the indulgent eyes of Satan (i. 604-12), and then at once provides an image which gives them the appearance of huge forest oaks, blasted but 'stately' too. Even when their superiority to men is frankly admitted the account is placed just after another passage in which

D

the metaphors, superbly handled, convey to us a widening sense
of their repulsive, indeed Neronic, cruelty: they have 'Rifl'd the
bowels' or 'womb' (673) of their new motherland, Hell, opening
there 'a spacious wound' and digging out 'ribs' of gold (684-90).
But these adumbrations of the devils' savagery and strength are
not exclusive. Other sides of their appearance and behaviour are
suggested in other passages, particularly towards the end of Book
One, and these too must be allowed for in any conception of them
which we are to entertain. There is, for example, the extra-
ordinary delicacy of the lines describing Mulciber's fall:

> From Morn
> To Noon he fell, from Noon to dewy Eve,
> A Summer's day; and with the setting Sun
> Dropt from the Zenith like a falling Star,
> On *Lemnos* th' *Ægæan* Ile.   (742-6)

There is also the sociable or industrious innocence (despite their
stings) conferred on the devils by the simile of the bees:

> As Bees
> In spring time, when the Sun with *Taurus* rides,
> Pour forth thir populous youth about the Hive
> In clusters; they among fresh dews and flowers
> Flie to and fro, or on the smoothed Plank,
> The suburb of thir Straw-built Cittadel,
> New rub'd with Baum, expatiate and confer
> Thir State affairs.   (768-75)

Both passages probably owe a good deal of their mollifying effect
to the Classics, the first because in it Milton is expressing indirectly
his delight in the 'dreams' and 'fancies' he more or less repudiates
elsewhere in both his epics, and the second because it is imitated
from the *Iliad*. But that they were left to stand can only mean that
the sidelight cast by them was felt to be relevant and necessary,
particularly since they are followed by another epic simile which
is not derived from the Classics and which is equally engaging.
Having shrunk, the devils are like

                    Faerie Elves,
        Whose midnight Revels, by a Forrest side
        Or Fountain some belated Peasant sees,
        Or dreams he sees, while over-head the Moon
        Sits Arbitress, and neerer to the Earth
        Wheels her pale course, they on thir mirth and dance
        Intent, with jocond Music charm his ear;
        At once with joy and fear his heart rebounds.   (781-8)

It is, surely, an equally complex 'fear' that Milton's readers are
meant to feel. The devils, like Satan, are not to be simplified and
circumscribed, but must be allowed the fullness of their own
intrinsic life. It is not for us to take away what the poet has given.

                                II
    Certain initial difficulties again arise with the Great Consult in
Book Two, and even perhaps with its venue in Pandæmonium,
the devils' council chamber so fittingly likened to a Saracen arena
in which tests for Christian chivalry are devised (i. 763-6). The
account of its building is as assured a piece of verse as *Paradise Lost*
can show, and the structure has an air of reality about it that other
localities in the poem sometimes lack. But for that reason the
building is also finite in its dimensions, and this obliges Milton to
have his devils contract before they enter it: which in turn involves
some explanation of their ability to vary their form at will, an
explanation which is neither very apt nor quite in accord with
what we hear of the progressive degeneration in their appearance
(i. 591-2, ii. 304-5, iv. 838-40). Then too it is at first sight rather
odd that Satan should make even a pretence of democratic debate
in view of the devils' dread of his commands (ii. 473-5), and perhaps
odder still that a hothead like Moloch should make no reply to
Belial's taunting criticism of his proposals (ii. 178-83). Belial's
speech, too, seems to come from a more responsible sort of devil
than the one to whom we were introduced at i. 490-505.
    Such hesitations about the debate can best be set aside by assum-
ing, first, that even fallen angels are our superiors, with better
control of their egotisms than we usually have; and secondly, that

the characterizations in this part of the poem are in some sense conditional and tentative, the Consult representing a train of thought as well as an actual discussion. We have seen, during the catalogue of hero–devils and elsewhere in Book One, how close the artistic relation between Satan and his followers is, and must continue to think of it as close. This means that, though on one level the debate can be accepted as a debate, on another level it can also be accepted as a dramatized account of Satan's inner motives, much like the 'long debate, irresolute Of thoughts revolv'd' through which his mind is passing at ix. 87-8. Thus, when the Consult arrives at his conclusions, its members arrive at them in something of a double sense: both because his will has been imposed upon the assembly by Beelzebub, and because the debate has imitated the processes through which his own mind has been moving. This subjective dimension attributed to the Consult need not, however, be pressed too far, nor is it advisable to reduce the speakers to mere psychological figments. What individuality they possess can be readily accepted, and where it is lacking the lack need not seem serious. That is all.

The devils' meeting is solemn and imposing, like a sitting of some legendary Senate. Only the leaders of the infernal army attend, retaining their giant stature (i. 792-5), but since they are 'A thousand Demy-Gods' (796) we sense the vastness of the assembly and the almost infinite number of lesser devils who are excluded from it. Moreover, now that Satan is housed in his own palace his confidence increases, and his resounding apostrophes no longer tail off in regret (ii. 11-17). Yet along with these inflations, as before, Milton is careful to introduce discrediting or limiting touches too. In the opulent description of Satan with which the book begins one word, '*Barbaric*', spreads sly poison, and in his first speech there are equivocations which should warn us not to accept his statements too trustingly:

> From this descent
> Celestial vertues rising, will appear
> More glorious and more dread then from no fall,
> And trust themselves to fear no second fate.   (14-17)

Does 'to fear no second fate' mean 'not to be afraid of another failure, since we know now what failure entails', or does it mean 'to be confident of success now that our foe has been tested'? We do not know, and are reasonably sure that Satan himself does not know: his rhetoric is opaque and self-deluding. His logic, too, is incoherent. One good result of their fall from Heaven, he says, has been to confirm his leadership more authoritatively than was possible before (21-4)—cold comfort to his followers, one would think, for what they now endure—and yet in spite of this he still wants to return there (14).

With the devils' speeches the strange distinction they have acquired becomes less teasingly elusive, and less impressive, but then there is a more directly dramatic interest to make up for the loss. As is fitting the first speech is the least impressive. Moloch personifies the recklessness already seen in Satan, and like his leader he reveals a vast capacity for self-delusion, for inhabiting an unreal world where facts no longer matter. He believes, incredibly, that they may yet reconquer Heaven (60-4); he is fascinated by the thought of paying God back neatly in his own coin, thunder for thunder, fire for fire (64-70); and to justify his rashness he propounds a purely supposititious principle that it is their angelic nature to ascend, to gravitate upwards to Heaven (73-81). His eagerness to resume the War (92-101) is exactly like the eagerness of a patient demanding a dangerous operation because of an unreasonable conviction that it will restore him to perfect health: he has not really considered the possibility of its proving fatal, although he says he has. The speech reverberates in a limbo of unreality, and it peters out feebly as he adjusts himself belatedly to the real facts of their position (101-5). Any succeeding speech is likely to seem comparatively sane, but actually the speech of Belial's which follows is much more. There are minor inconsistencies in it, bred of resentment, like his questioning of the omnipotence which he later grants to God (153-4, 198), but otherwise it is bluntly realistic and sets out their predicament to a hair. Here something appears which will be troublesome later: a tendency in the poet to pass derogatory comments on the devils which are inadequately related to what he has presented. Milton's preliminary gibes at Belial for his hypocrisy (110-17) and his concluding remark about 'ignoble ease, and peaceful sloath' (227) would be justified if Belial still kept the character given him in Book One; but as things are the comments seem simply biased. Belial sees quite clearly the other alternative, total destruction, to which Moloch has shut his eyes (142-51), and unlike Beelzebub and Satan he is also aware of God's omniscience (190-3), the factor which renders all their plotting vain. His premises are correct and he deduces from them a perfectly feasible plan, on the face of it the only feasible plan still left apart from repentance, which is hardly feasible any longer. The others reject it, not because it is unrealistic, but because it fails to satisfy their hunger for revenge. Actually if anyone recommends 'ignoble ease, and peaceful sloath' it is Mammon, who follows Belial and takes his cue from him. His speech, like Moloch's, is again inferior but appropriately placed. For one thing, by restating Belial's argument crudely, and with a greedy emphasis on 'Gemms and Gold' (271), Mammon makes it seem less conclusive than it really is. For another, he shows how impossible for the devils repentance has now become (239-43). For yet another, by speaking grandiloquently of their preference for 'Hard liberty before the easie yoke Of servile Pomp' (256-7) he helps to restore some of their dignity and fascination, which the previous speeches, for different reasons, have perceptibly reduced. After he has spoken two things are clear: the devils, Moloch perhaps excepted, are not really eager to fight with God again; yet they hanker after some form of revenge. It is this indecision, of course, which makes Beelzebub's proposal so agreeable to the meeting, and Milton manages the sequel with great skill. Beelzebub, a far more commanding figure here than in Books One or Five, begins by pointing out that they are angels still, 'Thrones and Imperial Powers, off-spring of heav'n' (310), and at once our sense of their power comes flooding back. He answers Mammon tersely, for the moment persuading us that he has also answered Belial (317-23), and sets forth a plan which seems a perfect compromise between the two extremes of defiance and submission that have been urged. Indeed it is less a compromise than a conflation: while one delegate engages in a tit-for-tat repayment of God such as Moloch has advocated (362–76) the remainder of the army can pursue the line of lesser resistance recommended by Belial and Mammon. The flaw in all this is that Beelzebub, while granting God's omnipotence (324–6), has failed to recognize his omniscience, an error as we have seen that Belial does not make. But like the devils themselves we overlook his blunder in the quickening interest that follows the question 'What if we find Some easier enterprize?' (344–5), and it is only in Book Three that we are made to appreciate how inadequate the new plan may really be.

On the whole perhaps their speeches have reduced the devils' stature, if only because the artistic distance between them and ourselves has been decreased. Satan is the exception, since his opinions have been suggested indirectly. To restore our feelings of awe it is necessary now to vary the treatment, turning again to the leader of the host, and Milton proceeds to do this. Undercurrents of criticism naturally persist: Beelzebub speaks, for example, of the 'Great things' they have resolved when in fact their plan is a decidedly petty one (392). But the general effect of his lines describing the hazardous enterprise ahead is to make Satan almost as impressive to the reader as he is to his followers, and the devil's 'Monarchal pride' (428) will, after this, seem almost justified. Satan's own speech, as might be expected, minimizes neither his initiative nor his boldness (432–44), and when he addresses his men as 'mighty Powers, Terror of Heav'n' (456–7) they too recover some of their faded majesty. To be sure our hesitations are not abandoned. Reason tells us that the devils are Heaven's conquest, not its terror, and that Satan's obvious relish for the journey before him (465–6) belies Beelzebub's and his own attempts to represent it as a sheer ordeal. Indeed their diplomatic use of terms like 'feet' (404) and 'tread' (828) to make the crossing of the 'unbottom'd infinite Abyss' seem doubly heroic will be neatly riposted when later we learn that this is precisely how Satan has to proceed, 'Treading the crude consistence, half on foot' (941). Yet on the other hand a simile likens him to 'the radiant Sun' (492), the devils hold 'Firm concord' with each other in a way men cannot emulate (496-502), and Satan's state, if 'imitated', is also 'God-like' (511). It is clear that the ambivalences of Book One have not withdrawn, and that Hell still demands from the reader an attitude of suspended admiration, tinged with distaste and fear. The demand continues through the first half of the account of the devils' diversions which follows (521-628), an imitation of the fifth book of the *Aeneid* which again is something more than a simple imitation, but if we follow the drift attentively we cannot fail to notice that its real purpose is to reduce the devils' stature drastically. At first sight the diversions are heroic, like their classical equivalents, but Milton is also emphasizing the perplexed futility which they presuppose. The devils engage in sham-fights which, however fierce, are idle in view of their recent defeat and still more recent renunciation of force (531-8). They imitate the tactics of their late opponents in the Heavenly War, rending up rocks and hills (539-41), but an adroit simile makes clear that the imitation is senseless (542-6). Their angelic music, if ravishing, is 'partial' now (552), no longer tuned to the harmony of Heaven; and their philosophical discussions are little better than crossword puzzles, distractions to stave off consciousness (566-8). Finally we hear much of the dismal geography of Hell (570-95) and of the tortures of the damned (596-614). 'A Universe of death' is presented, a landscape made up of desolate and meaningless accretions:

> Rocks, Caves, Lakes, Fens, Bogs, Dens, and shades of death.   (621)

It is literally a case of one damned thing after another. Here 'everything exists, nothing has value': the purposes of the devils seem exhausted, and Hell takes on a lunar sterility.

Satan's own degradation is even more striking in what follows, though the lines raise artistic difficulties which the devils' diversions avoid. At first one is chiefly conscious of his intrepidity, the reference to his scouring one coast and then another (633) and the simile comparing his appearance to that of a merchant fleet

(636–42) combining with Beelzebub's earlier description of his journey as a quest for 'The happy Ile' (410) to make a navigator of him, a contemporary sea-discoverer. Then too the encounter with Sin and Death does not at once discredit him:

> Th' undaunted Fiend what this might be admir'd,
> Admir'd, not fear'd; God and his Son except,
> Created thing naught valu'd he nor shun'd. (677–9)

But very soon the relationships between the unholy trio are made clear, and Satan's depravity emerges more clearly with them. Two points need to be made about this section of the poem. In the first place Sin and Death are allegorical abstractions in a much fuller sense than Satan and his devils are, so that some adjustment is required in the attention we have been giving. To a poet like Milton, whose neo-Platonic tendencies are almost as pronounced as Shelley's (consider the revealing use of 'ti'd', 'manacl'd', and other weighted words at i. 424–8), this new level is not inferior to what has gone before. To ourselves, however, poetry and dramatic interest are likely to seem far more closely involved with 'cumbrous flesh' than with an 'Essence pure' (cf. again 424–8), and Sin and Death in turn are likely to seem far less poetically interesting than Adam, Beelzebub, or even God. As Dr. Johnson said, they are unreal, and to attribute actions to them is 'to shock the mind by ascribing effects to non-entity'.[1] At any rate, if no longer shocked, the mind is disengaged. In the second place the allegory is by no means an unqualified success, much of it being downright confused, or at least confusing. True, it ensures a number of effects that are striking and occasionally important. Satan's dislike of ugliness is revealed (745) which prepares us for his chagrin when told of his own at iv. 849–50; the 'darkness' and 'flames' attending Sin's birth (754) prefigure the Hell into which the devils have subsequently fallen; the degeneration that has taken place in Sin's appearance (783–5) implies a similar degeneration in Satan's; his love for her—a telling point—is shown to be self-love (764–5); the shameless opportunism of his flattery when

[1] *The Works of Samuel Johnson, LL.D.* (London, 1787), ii. 169 ('Life of Milton').

he calls Death 'my fair Son' (818) prepares us for his later flattery
of Eve; and in general he now takes on the lurid colours of Sin
and Death, the three together suggesting a ghastly parody of the
Holy Trinity (869). But these effects are bought at a heavy price,
for the allegory raises a host of questions that should never have
been raised at all. Why, if all three are united in their hostility
to God (730-6), should Death's first speech to Satan be so censorious (689-703), a replica of the reproving speeches of Ithuriel,
Zephon, and Gabriel in Book Four? Why, in view of his utter
disregard for Sin (790-809), should Death pay any attention to
her admonition to restrain his fury (734-5)? Why did God entrust
to Sin the key of Hell (774-5)? Does he foolishly expect her to
keep the gates locked, despite her obvious and avowed intention
(856-63) of disobeying him? Or is he less fool than knave, an
intriguer waiting to trap Satan—and perhaps Man too—after
they have been opened? Why (to revert to a previous criticism)
should Satan be admired for confronting Death 'Unterrifi'd'? If
Death need fear no 'living might' (855) does that entitle him to
discount the might of an immortal like Satan? As well as praising
him for giving her life (864-5) would Sin not feel resentful
towards Satan for giving her such a son? However arresting, is
it not a stark exaggeration to speak of the key to Hell's gates as
the 'Sad instrument of all our woe' (872)? And so on. Other
difficulties relating to the allegorical element in the poem will
appear in due course, but these alone are enough to show its
dangers.

Milton seems to escape with something like relief from the
trammels of these uncertainties. The description of Chaos which
follows is more poetically assured than anything in the encounter
with Sin and Death, and then comes the superb passage describing
Satan's launching into space:

> At last his Sail-broad Vannes
> He spreads for flight, and in the surging smoak
> Uplifted spurns the ground, thence many a League
> As in a cloudy Chair ascending rides
> Audacious, but that seat soon failing, meets

A vast vacuitie: all unawares
Fluttring his pennons vain plumb down he drops
Ten thousand fadom deep . . .   (927-34)

This is not only a vivid re-creation of physical movement, with
the flow and hesitation of the phrases closely imitating the swoop
and recoil and plunge of Satan's flight; it is also a striking symbolic
manifestation of Satan's ambitious pride and the discomfiture that
awaits it. But his impressiveness has been sufficiently curtailed and
in what follows Milton takes special pains to restore it, lest the
devil should seem merely contemptible. The train of imagery
relating him to an adventurous explorer reappears (958, 1011,
1043), and with it come allusions to the heroes of mythology,
Jason and Ulysses (1116-20). So too he is like 'a Pyramid of fire'
(1013)—ardour and strength coinciding, so to speak—and the
results he will achieve, despite the professorial qualification
Milton appends to them (1032-3), are felt to be prodigious.
Nowhere in the whole poem perhaps is Satan quite so impressive
as at the conclusion of Book Two, when his bulk is suspended
before the harmony and radiance of Creation, an enormous
shadow threatening the tiny, vulnerable globe of Earth. His wili-
ness during the Consult, Sin and Death, the difficulties of his
journey—all are momentarily forgotten. We see only the
monstrous silhouette approaching a small and seemingly defenceless star.

III

'Everybody feels', Waldock has commented, 'that the Satan of
the first two books stands alone; after them comes a break, and
he is never as impressive again. . . . It is not merely that the Satan
of the first two books re-enters altered: the Satan of the first two
books to all intents and purposes *disappears*.'[1] To speak of 'everybody' is rash, for Professor Lewis and Dr. Rajan feel no such
break and represent the Satan of the poem as undergoing a smooth

---

[1] *Paradise Lost and Its Critics* (Cambridge, 1947), pp. 81-2.

and even deflation, like a vast punctured balloon. 'From hero to general, from general to politician, from politician to secret service agent, and thence to a thing that peers in at bedroom or bathroom windows, and thence to a toad, and finally to a snake—such is the progress of Satan' says Lewis in a passage which seems to stick, inaccurately, in every student's memory; and Rajan adds that the decline, manifestly unchronological, 'is meant to be read poetically'.[1] Both views contain a higher proportion of truth than their flat dissent would lead one to expect, but neither seems to accord precisely with Satan's presentation in the remainder of the poem.

Let us take Waldock first. Almost everything he says in his fourth chapter is pertinent and acute, yet his contention that the figure which now confronts us 'is not a changed Satan, he is a *new* Satan'[2] goes some way beyond what the facts will warrant. To accept it one would need to overlook Milton's deflations of the devil during the first two books, and in particular one would have to forget Satan's association with Sin and Death. The view also implies that after Book Two Satan's stature is puny, or at any rate sadly reduced. Well, is it? In Book Three we watch him traversing a huge and 'windie Sea of Land' on foot, an explorer still (440-1); pausing dramatically to look down 'with wonder', and with silent menace, at the world below (540-51); plummeting down through space 'with ease' (561-5); landing in the brilliant incandescence of the sun (588) which leaves his eyes 'Undazl'd' (614); and misleading Uriel, 'The sharpest sighted Spirit of all in Heav'n', with his deft equivocations (662-7). So too in much of Book Nine we bear immediate witness to his irresistible persuasiveness and guile. No doubt these enhancements are qualified, and strictly qualified, by other incidents and observations, but when was Satan's magnificence ever unqualified? His environment is changing: we must expect the impression he makes to change with it. That is the implication of the phrase that comes

---

[1] C. S. Lewis, *A Preface to Paradise Lost* (O.U.P., 1942), p. 97; B. Rajan, *Paradise Lost and the Seventeenth Century Reader* (London, 1947), p. 105.

[2] *Paradise Lost and Its Critics*, p. 82.

at the beginning of Book Three, a touch which should not go unnoticed: 'In the dun Air sublime' (72). Only against a tenebrous backdrop of inferiority such as Hell provides is his stature still commanding, his radiance undimmed, and after leaving Hell he must inevitably encounter other backdrops which will dwarf and darken them. If there is a suggestion of tinsel theatricality about the disguise he puts on to deceive Uriel (iii. 640-4), if his behaviour on Mount Niphates is unheroic (iv. 114-17), if his glances now become sidelong and evasive (iv. 504, vi. 149), if the black magic of his disguise must yield to the white of Ithuriel's spear (iv. 810-14), if his bold speeches sometimes tail off in diplomatic qualification (iv. 854), these are not, surely, such unforeseen results as Waldock would make them out to be. Many of the deficiencies now attributed to him are really repetitions, only a little more emphatic, of deficiencies the reader has already detected: the egotism with which he relates all things to himself (iv. 508), the vanity which resents others seeing his impairment (iv. 849-50), the psychopathic detachment which provides him with his own false version of the War in Heaven (iv. 926-9), and the self-regard that admires Sin and Death's boldness or strength because he can equate it with his own (x. 389-91, 404-5). The rhetoric that was self-deluding in Book Two is equally opaque in Book Four, equally but no more:

> Hence I will excite thir minds
> With more desire to know, and to reject
> Envious commands, invented with designe
> To keep them low whom knowledge might exalt
> Equal with Gods; aspiring to be such,
> They taste and die: what likelier can ensue? (iv. 522-7)

Does Satan know, we wonder, how much of this relates to his own reaction, 'Knowledge forbidd'n? Suspicious, reasonless' (515-16), and how much is simply a rehearsal of the arguments he will present to Adam or Eve? Can commands be merely 'Envious' if, transgressed, the offenders 'taste and die'? Even his deformed appearance as a toad (800) and Gabriel's characterization of him as a 'sly hypocrite' who 'Once fawn'd, and cring'd, and servilly ador'd' in Heaven (957-9) are not entirely unexpected: it was already apparent that he would go to any lengths to prosecute his ends, and equally apparent that his account of his fall from Heaven was untrustworthy. We do violence to the poem if we say that there are two identities in Satan rather than one.

This would seem to leave only the alternative view that Lewis and Rajan hold. But it is hard to see how the smooth decline from hero to snake that Lewis describes can be made to fit the poem's facts, for the graph of Satan's history that it draws is very different from the bumpy and uncertain curve Milton provides. Who will maintain, for instance, that Satan is *less* impressive during the War in Heaven, or even the temptation, than he is at the perfunctory and anticlimactic conclusion of Book Four? Waldock was right to feel that some kind of clumsiness or neglect had set in after Book Two—or even earlier—and perhaps a distinction drawn will help to locate it. The figure of Satan is not, after all, identical with the treatment accorded him, and even if the devil remains unchanged Milton's treatment of him may have altered. Even a tolerant reader may call this straw-chopping, but it is less niggling than it sounds. The most striking thing about the treatment of Satan in the first two books, without a doubt, is its equivocality, the synthesis that is effected in a single figure between diverse and even contradictory qualities. More than anything else this renders him magnetic and stirs our imagination as we read. Is not the disappointment Waldock indicates the result, not of a metamorphosis in Satan himself, but of a deterioration and coarsening in Milton's technique? The question is all the more reasonable after Satan's appearances in Book Two. There, as we have seen, the ambiguity attributed to the devil in Book One has shown signs of breaking down, and already there have been glimpses less of complex colour than of alternate black and white: Satan undertaking the perilous journey to Earth, Satan encountering Sin and Death, and Satan poised against the tiny star.

Admittedly the ambiguous richness which he has had does not completely desert Satan in what succeeds. The simile in Book

Three comparing him to a vulture (431-9), for example, helps to preserve it, and his soliloquy on seeing Adam and Eve for the first time (iv. 358-92) is probably quite as equivocal in its effect as anything in Books One and Two. Here we are at first won over by the unwonted generosity of his reaction to their beauty (360-5), and in what follows there is an undertone of pity, touched with gentleness, of which we remain aware. Yet at the same time we feel the incongruity of Satan's pity when it is extended to his victims (366-73), and can detect the self-pity that goes with it (373-5), a self-pity that becomes insincerity with his almost jocular offer to 'entertain' the human pair in Hell (375-87). The mere tone of the speech is enough to show complexity in the speaker: a perhaps genuine compassion, and an ability to dramatize it into something counterfeit. These reversions to the manner of the opening books, however, are sporadic and exceptional. In the majority of the passages now given to Satan Milton's treatment has become much less inclusive, and the colour and excitement previously associated with him have almost disappeared. It is partly a matter of the distance between him and ourselves having lessened, as with the devils during the Consult, so that he seems more ordinary and accessible, a figure almost of flesh and blood. When he approaches Uriel, for instance, the angel overhears his footsteps much as human footsteps might be overheard (iii. 645-7). But there is more to it than that. Milton's own attitude to the devil seems to have altered, as if he could no longer bear to hold it poised but had to come down on one side or the other, with praise or blame. One observes how explicit his comments on Satan have become, how anxious he seems to underline the devil's faults. Often this leads to intrusively disparaging comments (iii. 630, iv. 393-4, iv. 536), or to comments which are so unrelated to what has been presented that they seem almost malicious (iv. 902, vi. 787-8). The point can be illustrated by his remarks on the speech with which Satan deceives Uriel in Book Three, where at first he calls Satan 'the false dissembler' (681), a fair and reasonable rebuke, and then 'the fraudulent Impostor foule' (692), a phrase that sounds gratuitously abusive. Waldock has commented

perceptively on what he calls these 'automatic snubs', but he has
not noticed that in the opening books they are an integral part
of Milton's method.[1] Only later do they seem automatic, because
they are dissociated and overemphasized. Consider another
example, Satan's soliloquy on Mount Niphates. This credits the
devil with 'horror and doubt' regarding his plot to bring about
the Fall of Man (iv. 18), with a 'conscience' (23), with self-
knowledge (96-101), and with a jealousy of Man that is rather
more latent, requiring almost an effort to quicken it (105-7),
than earlier passages have led us to expect (ii. 349-50, ii. 370-6,
iii. 677-80). It is understandable that an archangel like Uriel
should later condemn such feelings as 'passions foul' (iv. 571)—to
him they are—but when Milton himself springs forward at the
end of the soliloquy to call them 'distempers foule' (118) he seems
dull and censorious, his own presentation having rendered Satan
less 'foule' than incoherent, and very nearly pitiable. What is
happening is clear. The complexity which Satan had is decom-
posing: qualities that were fused in him are beginning to alternate,
to move apart. Even the positive qualities that he had are sometimes isolated to show their moral inadequacy, as when Raphael
explains that

> strength from Truth divided and from Just,
> Illaudable, naught merits but dispraise
> And ignominie.   (vi. 381-3; cf. vi. 820-1)

Then too only in the later books is anything like a sharp line
drawn between the public and the private Satan, at first by
implication during the Mount Niphates soliloquy (iv. 82-3), and
later more clearly when he puts on an air of 'scorn' to cover the
mortification he feels before Ithuriel and Zephon (iv. 827, 846-51).
During his encounter with the two sentries an alternation of
private and public *personae* is plain to see:

> The Fiend repli'd not, overcome with rage;
> But like a proud Steed reind, went hautie on,
> Chaumping his iron curb: to strive or flie

---

[1] *Paradise Lost and Its Critics*, pp. 78-81.

> He held it vain; awe from above had quelld
> His heart, not else dismai'd.   (iv. 857-61)

This is not the integration in a single form of majesty and evil;
it is merely a description of pretence. A degree of expediency has
appeared in Milton's presentation which was not there before. It
reappears, though altered, in the lines applied to Satan a little
later, when Gabriel and he are face to face:

> On th' other side *Satan* allarm'd
> Collecting all his might dilated stood,
> Like *Teneriff* or *Atlas* unremov'd:
> His stature reacht the Skie, and on his Crest
> Sat horror Plum'd . . . .   (985-9)

By itself this might be the figure of the first two books returned,
but the pejorative touches—'dilated' (like the toad he was), and
'horror'—are much more overt and tend to flatten it, reducing
Satan to a cardboard silhouette. One feels that Milton has seized
the chance to dramatize the confrontation, but nothing more.
And when just afterwards one of the most significant qualities
that Satan has is suddenly abandoned, his habitual disregard for
facts (cf. 928, 973), the poet's opportunism is even more blatant:

> The Fiend lookt up and knew
> His mounted scale aloft: nor more; but fled
> Murmuring.   (1013-15)

Would the Satan previously revealed to us, opposed by a detachment as unimpressive as Gabriel's has become, and by a symbolic
demonstration in the sky, behave in any such fashion? For the
moment Waldock's interpretation is the simple truth: 'he is not a
changed Satan, he is a *new* Satan'. Worst of all, he is a Satan from
whom all real interest has drained away.

One further aspect of the deterioration in Milton's treatment of
the devil must be mentioned: the loss of poetic energy or resonance in the heroic similes applied to him. These play a very
important part in determining the reader's impressions during
the opening books, where they are consistently good and often
masterly, but the similes of the succeeding books, though they

E

recover their potency in Book Nine, are usually far less effective. Almost any example might be taken from Book One to show how the impression left by Satan or his devils is quickened and enlarged: the comparison with Leviathan (200-8), the Etna simile (230-7), the splendid series beginning 'Thick as Autumnal Leaves' (302-13), the comparison with lightning-blasted trees (612-15), the Organ simile applied to the effortless rising of Pandæmonium (708-9), or the similes of the bees and elves. I take a representative instance not so far mentioned:

> His form had yet not lost
> All her Original brightness, nor appear'd
> Less then Arch Angel ruind, and th' excess
> Of Glory obscur'd: As when the Sun new ris'n
> Looks through the Horizontal misty Air
> Shorn of his Beams, or from behind the Moon
> In dim Eclips disastrous twilight sheds
> On half the Nations, and with fear of change
> Perplexes Monarchs. Dark'n'd so, yet shon
> Above them all th' Arch Angel.   (591-600)

Observe how smoothly the 'or' of line 596 combines the pleasant warmth and freshness of a rising sun with the portentous gloom and augury of a sun eclipsed, and observe the clashes and collocations in the diction: 'brightness . . . ruind . . . excess Of Glory obscur'd . . . Sun . . . misty . . . Beams . . . Moon . . . disastrous twilight . . . Dark'n'd . . . shon.' Here Satan's ambivalence is compressed into ten lines, yet with no sacrifice in its richness. In the same way the similes in Book Two are often crowded with apt connotations (285-90, 542-6), and it is only in the second half of the book that there is any falling off in their quality or their aptness:

> . . . Such a frown
> Each cast at th' other, as when two black Clouds
> With Heav'ns Artillery fraught, come rattling on
> Over the *Caspian*, then stand front to front
> Hov'ring a space, till Winds the signal blow
> To joyn thir dark Encounter in mid air.   (713-18)

With its excessive emphasis on a frown this anticipates the several
enfeebled similes and comparisons of Book Four, though no one
would argue that it is as forced as the first of them:

> So entertaind those odorous sweets [of Paradise] the Fiend
> Who came thir bane, though with them better pleas'd
> Then *Asmodeus* with the fishie fume,
> That drove him, though enamourd, from the Spouse
> Of *Tobits* Son . . . . (vi. 166-70)

Since in the Book of Tobit Asmodeus was driven away by the
fishy smell, which was rank and unpleasant, it is inconceivable
that Satan would be otherwise than 'better pleas'd' with the
odours of the Garden. All that the allusion does is to establish
a random connexion between two evil spirits. So also the two
similes that follow, relating Satan to a wolf leaping into a sheep-
fold and to a burglar entering a house (iv. 183-91), though they
are often praised, have little of the inspired appropriateness of the
similes in Book One. The first is humdrum, and the second, with
its suggestion of smug incompetence on the part of the householder, tends to reflect adversely on Gabriel, Adam, and even
God. Nor can one make more of it by pretending, in the teeth
of the evidence, that it is humorous, as Dr. Tillyard does.[1] Later
in Book Four the quality of the similes improves (e.g. 556-60),
but when the focus returns to Satan they fall off again, as in the
example already mentioned, comparing the spears of Gabriel's
sentries to bending ears of corn and Satan (apparently) to a
ploughman (980-5). And even in Book Six there are examples of
unsteady connotation, as in the simile which likens Satan to a
displaced mountain, thus at the same time awkwardly relating
Abdiel, his assailant, to some kind of terrestrial eruption:

> Ten paces huge
> He back recoild; the tenth on bended knee
> His massie Spear upstaid; as if on Earth
> Winds under ground or waters forcing way
> Sidelong, had push't a Mountain from his seat
> Half sunk with all his Pines. (193-8)

---

[1] E. M. W. Tillyard, *Studies in Milton* (London, 1951), pp. 74-5.

Such similes have only to be compared with those in Books One and Nine: this done, their inferiority is obvious. It is an inferiority that transmits itself to the figure of Satan also, and it goes far to account for the disappointment Waldock has indicated.

IV

Perhaps the argument can be pushed one stage farther before we leave it. In view of the Satanist propensity for identifying Milton's treatment of Satan with his own psychology a very important reason for the devil's decline, though a hidden one, should also be mentioned. The Satanists have had, on the whole, a more serious hearing than their contentions merit, and this in turn has meant that the figure of Satan, like that of Hamlet, has almost disappeared under a mountain of commentary. Occasionally one can point out arguments in their favour which they themselves have missed. Milton's phraseology at the beginning of Book Three, for instance, might seem on the face of it to make a closer link between the devil and himself than has been observed: like Satan, he proceeds 'with bolder wing' (13), escaping into 'flight' after an 'obscure sojourn' (15). But the speculative opportunity such phrases provide is a specious one: they cut no ultimate ice whatever. On the other hand it is not always easy to refute the Satanist case incisively, because to do so requires a more discerning attitude to the problems of narrative or dramatic technique than can be readily assumed. Vondel, however, again provides an analogy that is relevant to *Paradise Lost*, and one which clarifies the point I wish to make. Let us consider two speeches given to his Lucifer.

The first is this, from the second act of *Lucifer*, where the angel is discussing with Belzebub what they take to be God's plan to elevate Man at their expense:

> You are discerning: it ill befits a ruler
> Worthy to rule so to let slip prerogatives
> Vested in him. Supremacy must be bound
> By its own laws, immutable and constant.

If I am Son and Ruler of the Light
I shall defend my rights. I cannot yield
Either to force or to an arch-usurper.
Let yield what will, I shall not flinch one foot;
Here is my domicile; neither disaster
Nor curses nor despair will curb or cow us;
We die, or else we round this dangerous cape.
If I must fall, robbed of my rank and honour,
I fall then—but with this crown upon my head,
This sceptre in my hand, this retinue
About me, and the thousands who take my side:
Such a defeat wins honour, immortal praise.
Better the prince of some inferior court
Than second, or less, in beatific light.
Defying fears, thus I accept my fate.[1]

The second speech is from *Adam in Ballingschap*. Lucifer speaks
after the Fall of Man:

Hell's turn it is to triumph at my revenge.
Let my ancestral enemy take precautions
To check this inroad of inveterate wrong:
No longer can the dams and weirs of law,
Of threats and promises, restrain or thwart me.
Created Nature lies abject, beaten, defiled:
The human race is mine, a vast inheritance,
Contemptuous now of promises and threats,
Heedless of God, bent on depravity.
I too, in his despite, will found my churches,
My image will be revered with gold and incense
And human sacrifice; and men will fear me
And swear by me. I shift from my own neck
To God's, deceitfully, the weight of sin.
Through sixty centuries teeming with Adam's children
Scarcely a handful will God's power redeem.
Thus am I elevated by my own decline,
Thus does an apple tasted bring me strength.[2]

---

[1] See passage C in the Appendix.   [2] Passage D in the Appendix.

The temptation, when the two extracts are compared, is to ascribe their differences in tone and suggestion simply to the fact that Lucifer's fall has intervened between them, to say that the first shows the integrity and determination of a heavenly spirit and the second the pride and malice of a devil. This is partly true, but it oversimplifies the speeches and their force in the dramatic context where each occurs. In *Lucifer* the protagonist is not just unfallen. He is, as it were, depicted from within, comprehended in much the same fashion as a tragic hero, and our feelings are often identified with his. Though Vondel has clearly indicated the limits of his greatness they are not so constricting as to exclude our attention and sympathy. We see his point of view, we understand his indignation, and in a way we even fall with him. In *Adam in Ballingschap*, however, all this has changed. Lucifer has become furtive and vainglorious, an enemy, and his associates are now a set of shady and malign conspirators. Their methods, once so direct and forthright, Lucifer himself calls 'deceit, and cunning, and clandestine ambush' (*bedrogh, en list, en heimelijcke laegen*); their purpose, once so easily justified as an enforcement of prerogative, a holy war, is now mere *beeldeschenderye*, the sacrilegious desecration of God's image in Man.[1] It is not only a matter of the devils having fallen and thus renounced their celestial dignity. Over and above their fall there is a marked withdrawal of the poet's sympathy from them, a new and hostile coolness in his appraisal.

The crucial point about this change in Vondel's attitude is that in *Lucifer* all the characters are angels, whether or not of the devil's party, whereas in *Adam in Ballingschap* the two chief characters are human beings. The presence of Adam and Eve has polarized the poet's attitude towards the devils, and now prevents him from identifying himself with them to the extent that he found possible in the earlier play. It is a result which any writer who has aspired beyond lyric or monologue might have predicted. Set a single character on the stage and, even if he is your villain, you may

---

[1] *Adam in Ballingschap*, 561 and 574.

commit yourself to his viewpoint as fully as you like. But let another figure enter, a figure whose claims upon you are compelling, whose claims must be clear, and at once your relationship with the first is disturbed. A master dramatist, a Shakespeare or Vondel, can still admit the claims of villainy in such a situation, provided the two characters are comfortable and in their way equivalent. Iago is not unrecognizably reduced by Othello's presence, and Lucifer, in Vondel's earlier play, preserves his stature in the presence of Rafaël. But when the characters exist on different planes, the villain a spirit and his opponent a human being, the effort required for impartiality becomes not only excessive but impolitic. In such a case to give the devil his due is to risk the human audience's displeasure. It is rather as if a man were to be introduced into one of Aesop's fables, and represented as a pathetic victim. The reader could not be blamed if his sympathies gravitated towards this unfortunate, a version of himself, rather than towards the lion or wolf who got the upper hand. Nor could the fabulist afford to ignore the likelihood that this would happen. It would be very likely to happen to him as well.

This polarization by human contact has been at work just as strongly in *Paradise Lost* as in Vondel's plays, and by itself it is probably a sufficient explanation why, especially after the end of Book Three, Satan's appearance should seem so shrunken and his behaviour so ignoble in comparison with what they were in the opening books. Indeed I think a whole train of such polarizations can be traced in the development of the poem, with the comparatively human figure of Satan in Books One and Two polarizing the more remote figure of God in Book Three (where the Son is also a polarizing agent), being polarized himself by the human figures of Book Four, who in their turn polarize the visitor Raphael and are perhaps partly polarized by the man-angel Michael in Book Eleven. It seems unnecessary to resort to conjectures about Milton's unconscious mind, and censoring consciousness, when a comparatively objective factor like this can be seen working to Satan's detriment. Our main task, in any case, is not to conjecture but to assess what is presented. This, as I say, neither Waldock's theory of a metamorphosis nor Lewis's theory of a smooth decline, for all their plausibility, seems quite to accomplish. A better account of Satan's progress in the poem would be to say that he is progressively simplified. A wonderfully iridescent surface, shot with conflicting lights, is subject to a gradual arrest, in the process coming more and more to resemble a mosaic crudely patterned with dark and light. Dramatic intensity, once located within the figure of Satan, has shifted elsewhere, and Milton's artistry has shifted with it.

Chapter Four

THE WAR IN HEAVEN

I

WHAT prompts the rebellion of Satan and his angels? The poet's chief authority for the War in Heaven was Revelation 12: 7-9, but this says nothing of Satan's motives for rebelling, which must be inferred from other texts in the Bible or its commentaries. There were at least five accounts from which Milton was free to choose and before going any farther it will be convenient to list them.

(1) There is first of all the biblical inference that Satan wished to emulate God, and perhaps even equal Him. Such at least is the deduction which was drawn, by a feat more of zeal than of logic, from Ezekiel's comments on the King of Tyre (28: 12-15) and, more especially, from Isaiah's complaint against the King of Babylon: 'How art thou fallen from heaven, O Lucifer, son of the morning! how art thou cut down to the ground, which didst weaken the nations! For thou hast said in thine heart, I will ascend into heaven, I will exalt my throne above the stars of God: I will sit also upon the mount of the congregation, in the sides of the north: I will ascend above the heights of the clouds; I will be like the most High. Yet thou shalt be brought down to hell, to the sides of the pit' (14: 12-15).

(2) Next there is the adaptation of this account which Milton used, where Satan's jealousy is directed less against God Himself than against His Son. The usual misinterpretations being allowed for, biblical warrants for such an adaptation are not hard to find, notably in two verses of the first chapter of St. Paul's Epistle to the Hebrews: 'For unto which of the angels said he at any time, Thou art my son, this day have I begotten thee? . . . When he bringeth in the firstbegotten into the world, he saith, And let all the angels of God worship him' (5-6).

(3) Thirdly, there is an early Hebrew account which represents the fall of the angels as a consequence of their lustful union with human females. This view derives in part from the second verse of Genesis 6: 'The sons of God saw the daughters of men that they were fair; and they took them wives of all which they chose', a text in which 'the sons of God' was later reinterpreted to mean 'the sons of judges and magistrates'. Milton, like later Hebrew commentators, apparently interpreted the passage as referring to men rather than angels, as in the account of the corruption of the Sethites in Book Eleven of *Paradise Lost*, where he says that it was their 'lives Religious [that] titl'd them the Sons of God' (621-2).[1]

(4) Fourthly, there is an account which attributes the angels' fall to their resentment at the promise of the Incarnation, the projected union between the Son of God and their inferior, Man. This seems to derive from the treatise *De Angelis* by the Catholic commentator Suarez. To judge from the seventh chapter of Antonia White's novel *Frost in May* it was still quite recently a common view among Catholics, though it is not really compatible with the Thomist position that the Incarnation was a consequence of Adam and Eve's sin. As *The Catholic Encyclopedia* points out (s.v. *Devil*): 'Since the sin [of our first parents] itself was committed at the instigation of Satan, it presupposes the fall of the angels. How, then, could Satan's probation consist in the foreknowledge of that which would, *ex hypothesi*, only come to pass in the event of his fall?' The argument becomes teleological if we say that Satan fell because the consequences of his fall were such as to arouse his jealousy.

(5) Lastly, there is the motivation which Vondel provides for the rebel angels in *Lucifer*, perhaps a modification of the preceding account. According to this the angels resented acting as servants to Man, and felt that God was disturbing the hierarchical order of creation by requiring their service. The idea is set forth in Lucifer's first speech in the play:

> Mankind has won the heart of the most High
> In the new Paradise: heaven's amity is theirs:

---

[1] In *Milton and the Angels* (University of Georgia Press, 1955, pp. 129-31) Robert H. West has shown that other passages in Milton's epics (P.L. v. 446-50, P.R. ii 173-81) are not incompatible with this passage, as was formerly supposed. But this is not to deny that Milton *could* have used the earlier interpretation as a basis for *Paradise Lost* if he had wanted to.

Our servitude begins. Go in obedience,
Honour the new race like subjected vassals, &c.[1]

It appears in *Paradise Lost* also, but only as a passing rationalization in the soliloquy of Satan at the beginning of Book Nine:

Man he made, and for him built
Magnificent this World, and Earth his seat,
Him Lord pronounc'd, and, O indignitie!
Subjected to his service Angel wings,
And flaming Ministers to watch and tend
Thir earthy Charge.   (152-7)

The chief point to bear in mind about these diverse accounts is that all were equally available to Milton, and that there was no constraint upon him to follow one or the other. As Professor Hughes has said, 'His whole poem rests upon the assumption that the devils were expelled from heaven before the creation of the universe, yet in the *Christian Doctrine* he questions the point. One Hebrew tradition has it that the devils fell because they were tempted by the beauty of the daughters of men. If it had suited his purpose, we may be sure that Milton would have adopted that legend.'[2] There was no doctrinal impediment between any of the five interpretations and his own beliefs, not even in the case of the fourth. The implication must be, then, that he chose his interpretation on artistic grounds only, and in fact this is usually conceded. 'It suited his scheme to open his poem with a council of the infernal angels', and he preferred the view that the fall of the angels preceded the creation of the world, and of Man, because 'it permitted Satan's quest of the new universe through Chaos'.[3] It is thus advisable, when we examine the motivation for the War in Heaven, to consider it in connexion with the artistic rather than the doctrinal problems which it involves. What are the artistic

---

[1] *Lucifer*, 361 ff.: De menschen hebben 't hart des Oppersten gewonnen,
In 't nieuwe Paradys: de mensch is 's hemels vrient:
Ons slaverny gaet in. gaet hene, viert, en dient,
En eert dit nieuw geslacht, als onderdane knapen, &c.
[2] *Paradise Lost*, ed. Merritt Y. Hughes (New York, 1935), p. xxvi.
[3] Ibid. pp. xxvi-vii, 33 n.

consequences in the poem of Milton's choice of the second interpretation rather than one of the other four?

So far as God is concerned Milton's version raises immediate difficulties. Its effect is actually twofold, for it represents God as an arbitrary and curiously assertive ruler, and in doing so tends to shift some of our sympathy—a good deal more than Milton ever intended—to Satan's cause. We have witnessed, in Book Three, God's elevation of his Son:

> All Power
> I give thee, reign for ever, and assume
> Thy Merits; under thee as Head Supream
> Thrones, Princedoms, Powers, Dominions I reduce.　(317-20)

This is not in any way prospective, retrospective, or conditional: God is appointing his Son as the ruler of the angels then and there, immediately, as his words and their reaction (344 ff.) both make plain. But two books later, or about three weeks earlier (depending on how one chooses to look at it), he seems, in so far as his statement is intelligible at all, to be doing very much the same thing:

> This day I have begot whom I declare
> My onely Son, and on this holy Hill
> Him have anointed, whom ye now behold
> At my right hand; your Head I him appoint;
> And by my Self have sworn to him shall bow
> All knees in Heav'n, and shall confess him Lord.　(v. 603-8)

The use of 'begot' here was something of a crux for expositors until Sir Herbert Grierson pointed out that it had to be accepted in a metaphorical rather than a literal sense.[1] Since the Son is said to have created the angels (iii. 390-1, v. 835-40) it is obviously impossible for his literal begetting to take place as late as this, so that the word must have the force of 'elevated' or 'brought forward as official leader'. But even if this interpretation is approved, as I think it must be, the passage is still a very difficult one to accept with full emotional compliance in the context where it comes. Raphael says nothing of the reasons which prompted

---

[1] *Milton and Wordsworth* (Cambridge, 1938), p. 99.

God to make his declaration—what can an angel know of them?—
and in consequence it seems impulsive, arbitrary, and even auto-
cratic. I do not mean that we dispute God's right to publish such
a statement. But we feel that the Son's pre-eminence must be
perfectly clear to all the angels, and that God's speech is an
unnecessary attempt to dot Heaven's i's and cross its t's, the act
of a legalistic quibbler rather than a divinity. Again, if the Son's
pre-eminence is not a matter of general acceptance, as Satan's
reaction might be held to prove, would not omniscience have
sense enough to explain the point more lucidly? Why should God
suddenly summon all his angels, thrust the decision upon them,
and then dismiss them like so many worthless underlings? It is as
though he were deliberately seeking to precipitate a rebellion, by
rudely challenging their legitimate self-esteem. Then too, because
of the preceding (or succeeding) elevation in Book Three, God's
generosity to his Son seems curious. Why *two* attempts to promote
him, especially when in each case he is promoted to the same rank?
When Satan tells his men that God is merely demanding 'Knee-
tribute' from them (v. 782) we cannot avoid the suspicion that
there is something in what he says. It has all been too abrupt, or
quite unnecessary.

What of the rebellious angels themselves meanwhile? Though
God's promotion of his Son can be plausibly represented as a
motive for Satan's personal rebellion, it surely provides no motive
at all for the rebellion of his hundreds of thousands of followers.
A military analogy helps to make this clear. Satan's followers,
we may say, are privates in one of God's regiments, and they have
been informed by God, their general, that his Son is now their
colonel, whom they must obey. However irritating this may be to
Satan, still a major along with Michael and Gabriel, would it be
any more than a matter of indifference to the men?—unless
indeed the new colonel was known to be a detestable martinet, a
supposition which is nowhere advanced and which would have
been flagrantly improbable if it had been. It is conceivable that
Satan 'thought himself impair'd' by the Son's elevation to an
apparently higher rank (v. 665), but that the rebellious angels are

also 'aspiring to his highth' (vi. 793) is surely incredible. Milton's task in Book Five, accordingly, is somehow to generalize and extend the motivation he has provided for Satan until it can be felt to include his followers as well. The Son's assertion later, 'against mee is all thir rage' (vi. 813), must have some colour of plausibility when it comes. The task is an extremely difficult one to accomplish satisfactorily, yet Milton seems almost indifferent to the difficulty. After telling us of Satan's reaction to the divine announcement, he reports a vague speech of provocation to Beelzebub (v. 673-93), and after that we are obliged to believe that Beelzebub has been converted to Satan's point of view (694-6). What, we ask, has happened to the intuitive reason which, in common with the other angels (488-9), he enjoys? What indeed has happened to the sage and deliberate counsellor we glimpsed (ii. 299-309) during the Great Consult? Beelzebub, passing on Satan's orders, 'casts between Ambiguous words and jealousies, to sound Or taint integritie' (v. 702-4), but obviously the onus is still on Satan to persuade his legions of the justice of his cause. Milton tries to conceal the fact that this is so by speaking of their obedience (704) and of their being 'banded to oppose [God's] high Decree' (717), but it is clear from Satan's orders to Beelzebub that their obedience only lies in carrying out the order to assemble, and that, far from being 'banded to oppose', they are in fact assembling, as they think, 'to prepare Fit entertainment to receive [thir] King The great *Messiah*' (689-91). A little later Milton has to admit that they are unsuspecting, and that it rests with Satan's 'calumnious Art' to persuade them to rebel (768-70). In view of this admission it is advisable to quote the whole of Satan's speech, thirty-one lines, by which, we are to understand, the persuasion was achieved:

> Thrones, Dominations, Princedomes, Vertues, Powers,
> If these magnific Titles yet remain
> Not meerly titular, since by Decree
> Another now hath to himself ingross't
> All Power, and us eclipst under the name
> Of King anointed, for whom all this haste

Of midnight march, and hurried meeting here,
This onely to consult how we may best
With what may be devis'd of honours new
Receive him coming to receive from us
Knee-tribute yet unpaid, prostration vile,
Too much to one, but double how endur'd,
To one and to his image now proclaim'd?
But what if better counsels might erect
Our minds and teach us to cast off this Yoke?
Will ye submit your necks, and chuse to bend
The supple knee? ye will not, if I trust
To know ye right, or if ye know your selves
Natives and Sons of Heav'n possest before
By none, and if not equal all, yet free,
Equally free; for Orders and Degrees
Jarr not with liberty, but well consist.
Who can in reason then or right assume
Monarchie over such as live by right
His equals, if in power and splendor less,
In freedome equal? or can introduce
Law and Edict on us, who without law
Erre not, much less for this to be our Lord,
And look for adoration to th' abuse
Of those Imperial Titles which assert
Our being ordain'd to govern, not to serve?   (772-802)

Satan's other arguments, when they come, are really attempted
refutations of the objections Abdiel raises: the core of his case is
here. Surely when we bear in mind what mountains these words
must move, or even when we compare them with Belial's or
Beelzebub's during the Consult, the utter inadequacy of the
speech is plain? Belial's and Beelzebub's speeches, after all, are
addressed to the clouded minds of fallen angels: the probative
force required from them is comparatively weak. This speech is
delivered to a vast assembly of crystal-clear intelligences. Are we
to believe that its blatant misrepresentations (775-6) and self-
confutations (792-3) are apparent only to a single auditor, the
zealous Abdiel? Worse, are we to believe that when Abdiel has

pointed out the fallacies in Satan's position, being accorded nine
additional lines to do it (809-48), the angels can make no more of
his words than that they are unseasonable, 'Or singular and rash'
(851)? Let it be remembered that these are the same angels whose
intelligence and tactical independence in battle is later admiringly
reported (vi. 232-6), who are still 'upright And faithful' (vi. 270-1),
whose prescience, like the unfallen Zophiel's later, is as yet quite
unimpaired (vi. 544-6). How, after all that Raphael and Milton
himself have conveyed to us concerning the natural capacity of
angels, are we to conceive of them inviting their own destruction
on grounds as dubious as Satan has advanced? It may be retorted
that the rebels expected to win, as Milton several times makes
clear (i. 93-4, vi. 86-8). What warrant had they then for doing so?
On the face of it such an expectation is patently absurd. As
Abdiel says: 'Fool, not to think how vain Against th' Omnipotent
to rise in Arms' (vi. 135-6). Fool indeed, and the folly passes all
bounds of credibility when it is extended to innumerable
'Myriads' (i. 622), to an army whose leaders alone are called 'A
thousand Demy-Gods' (i. 796). Has Satan somehow contrived to
isolate Heaven's imbeciles, and is a third of its population im-
becilic? Or are Milton's suggestions elsewhere (i. 680-4, iv. 957-61)
that the angels were fallen before their fall quite seriously intended?
What, in either case, does that make God?

It is no use arguing that to read with this degree of intentness
is to read the poem amiss. The poet himself has conditioned the
degree of our intentness with his persistent explanations and interpretations, to which it has become adjusted. If it was necessary
to explain the digestive processes of angels a little earlier (v. 407-
43) it is surely quite as necessary to explain the mental processes
which enable them to disregard Abdiel's admonitions here, and to
accept as gospel the rash assertions Satan hurls at them. Our basic
premise is identical with Adam's later:

> Suttle he needs must be, who could seduce
> Angels.   (ix. 307-8)

Yet at the time the best that Milton can do is to attribute Satan's
success to lies and to the brightness of his face:

His count'nance, as the Morning Starr that guides
The starrie flock, allur'd them, and with lyes
Drew after him the third part of Heav'ns Host. (v. 708-10)

It is said that the consequences of the rebellion were 'unforeseen,
unthought of' (ii. 821), but this is almost as incompatible with
angelic prescience as it is with the other assertion that they
expected to prevail. Nor is Satan's declaration that he was self-
created (v. 857-61) calculated to convince us that his oratory is
irresistible. We know that it is a lie (iv. 43) and are puzzled by the
angels' inability to refute it, if not from knowledge at least on
general grounds of probability. Like Raphael we ask, but with
sheer incredulity instead of wonder, 'In heav'nly Spirits could
such perverseness dwell?' (vi. 788). Even at its most stirring
(v. 864-9) Satan's appeal is manifestly inadequate to achieve its
ends, and our dismay to learn that he succeeds is in proportion.

Abdiel's presence, of course, does nothing to mitigate it. It
seems clear that much of Milton's personal independence, as a
writer and probably as a man, can be related to the notion of a
just man or angel defying the multitude and earning God's
approval. It haunted his imagination, appearing again and again
in what he wrote. The results are often artistically successful,
since in most cases (Enoch, Noah, Samson) his presentation is in
accord with the biblical material he is endeavouring to present,
and is in turn controlled by that material. Abdiel's intervention,
however, is controlled and confirmed neither by the Bible nor by
any other external authority. The angel is simply an opportunity
for Milton's wishful thoughts to express themselves, and the
impassioned verse describing his actions is enough to show how
closely the poet allowed himself to become involved:

So spake the Seraph *Abdiel* faithful found,
Among the faithless, faithful only hee;
Among innumerable false, unmov'd,
Unshak'n, unseduc'd, unterrifi'd
His Loyaltie he kept, his Love, his Zeale. (v. 896-900)

The idea is finely expressed, but Milton seems to have overlooked,
in his excitement at Abdiel's solitary defiance, the problem that

F

arises concerning all the other angels, whose loyalty, love, and zeal appear to have been recklessly mislaid. Abdiel has to be convincing, but the more convincing he is the more foolish, or wicked, the others must appear. If he knows that God is good (826) why are they in any doubt? Why cannot some at least make use of their intuitive reason to believe him, instead of Satan? Later it appears that he knew rather more about Satan's hopes and expectations than we ourselves were allowed to know (vi. 131-5). We wonder, if this is true, at his unwillingness to share the knowledge with his fellow-angels, in order to prevent their fall. The trouble is that plausibility has been sacrificed so as to permit the poet to dramatize a personal preoccupation, the one just character at bay before a multitude of the benighted or depraved.

Enough has been said to show how difficult it is to accept the opinion that Milton's treatment here is 'a real triumph of artistic handling', as one critic declares it to be.[1] The premises on which the War is made to rest are gravely mismanaged, and very little credence can be attached to them. Perhaps the point may be clinched by again referring to Vondel's *Lucifer*, where this does not happen. Since in the play the angels' impulse to rebellion is a general one, a jealousy of Man in which all can share, there is no necessity for them to be won over by their leader, and in fact the whole position is reversed, with Lucifer himself being persuaded by the Luciferists, already rebelliously inclined, to lead them in revolt (1183-1291). As one Dutch scholar has recently observed, 'The rebels try to force his hand by appealing to his pride, by compromising him, by placing him in a situation which he cannot back out of without losing face. . . . [And] step by step he lets himself be carried away.'[2] The relative advantages of such an approach are obvious. That one spirit could persuade a vast army of angels to follow his own deluded courses is inconceivable unless they fully shared his provocation; but that a vast army

---

[1] Arnold Williams, 'The Motivation of Satan's Rebellion in *Paradise Lost*', in *S.P.* xlii (1945), 268.

[2] W. A. P. Smit, 'The Emblematic Aspect of Vondel's Tragedies as the Key to their Interpretation', in *M.L.R.* lii (1957), 562.

could persuade their governor to lead them in an apparently righteous cause, his cause as well as theirs, is easy to believe. Vondel makes it all the more credible by elevating Lucifer to a rank immediately below God himself (423), so that his mistrust of God's authority and wisdom can seem more rational, and by showing how he is worked upon by Belzebub even before his encounter with the Luciferists (348-449). All in all, the effect is as plausible as any insurgency in Heaven very well can be. It is also the one kind of insurgency which would justify God's otherwise rather meaningless comment in *Paradise Lost* that the devils 'by thir own suggestion fell, Self-tempted, self-deprav'd' (iii. 129-30). One can argue that if Milton had chosen this motive Satan's quest through space might have been less adventurous, since presumably he would have had a more precise idea of his objective; but would so slight a loss in Book Two have outweighed the gain accruing in Book Five? Nor would the substitution have eliminated the faithful Abdiel, who could have been retained to speak for reason and duty just as Gabriël, Michaël, and the Chorus do in Vondel's play. The dramatic effectiveness of his opposition might then, indeed, have been quite unalloyed.

II

Milton offered the War in Heaven as a rough equivalent for the epic battles in the *Iliad* and the *Aeneid*. Like his occasional Homeric repetitions, like many of his heroic similes, or like the catalogue of heroes in Book One, it is a classical imitation, only more sustained. Still, as with his other imitations, it must be judged on its artistic merits, not for its relation to precedent. The critical problem is to decide whether it has the same inherent justification that the catalogue of heroes has, and that some of his repetitions also have (iv. 641-56, and xi. 261-2, which scrupulously repeats xi. 97-8)—whether it is functional and satisfying in itself—or whether on the contrary it is as mechanical as some of his other repetitions (iii. 402-5, and x. 1086-1104, where an effect possible in music miscarries) or as contrived as the device of the golden scales adapted from Homer to conclude Book Four. Very little light can be thrown on this decision by quoting comments like 'More safe I Sing' (vii. 24) or 'Not sedulous by nature to indite Wars' (ix. 27-8), for these are expressions of natural aptitude, not aesthetic verdicts. Difficulty may well have been as fascinating to Milton as, on his own admission, it was to Yeats. It is true that one or two other comments in the poem seem less irrelevant. Raphael's reluctance to describe what God has ordered him to describe (v. 563-70) and his frustration in the face of lifting 'Human imagination to such highth Of Godlike Power' (vi. 300-1) suggest that Milton found Book Six less stimulating to write than daunting; and Michael's belittling of Satan's physical defeat in comparison with his spiritual defeat through the Atonement (xii. 386-401) perhaps implies that the poet was less interested in the War than in the later stages of Satan's history. Here too, though, one is guessing about the process of composition rather than weighing what it achieved. The only method for determining Milton's success in the handling of his Homeric conflict is to examine Book Six with proper care.

One thing which soon appears is that Raphael has less of a talent for vivid narration than Milton himself has shown in preceding books. His story contains vestigial traces of a vigorous rhetoric, but they are traces only and lack the energy they once had:

> Hee together calls,
> Or several one by one, the Regent Powers,
> Under him Regent, tells, as he was taught,
> That the most High commanding, now ere Night,
> Now ere dim Night had disincumberd Heav'n,
> The great Hierarchal Standard was to move.   (v. 696-701)

Then, too, the angel relies heavily on assertive adjectives for his effects, a debilitating makeshift which the poem often uses, but especially here:

> 'Twixt Host and Host but narrow space was left,
> A dreadful intervall, and Front to Front
> Presented stood in terrible array
> Of hideous length.   (vi. 104-7)

Raphael's heroic similes, like the one comparing Satan to a displaced mountain (vi. 193-8), are sometimes rather extravagant, his parentheses are nearly always awkward (v. 580-2, 628-9; vi. 573-5, 640-1, 769), and he has little of the true storyteller's gift for holding his listener in forgetful suspense (vi. 90-1). It can be argued that some of these weaknesses arise only because he is translating unknowable experience for Adam's benefit, 'measuring things in Heav'n by things on Earth' (vi. 893). But if this is pressed too far one is obliged to question his ability as a translator and Adam's alertness as a listener, a reaction which is equally undesirable. In any case the narrative's weaknesses remain.

As to what is described, its interest is surely vastly inferior to the interest in Books One and Two, Book Four, or Book Nine. Book Six 'is, I believe, the favourite of children, and gradually neglected as knowledge is increased', wrote Johnson, and like so many of his observations on *Paradise Lost* the remark seems as perceptive today as it ever was.[1] The book would not be Milton's if it did not contain some good things: the touch relating Satan to an idol (101), the evocation of the noises of battle (207-14), the characterization of the devils as envious and self-seeking (498-9), and so on. But these cannot compensate for all the intervening crudities, or for what Johnson called 'the confusion of spirit and matter which pervades the whole narration'. The comment is acute. Raphael's discussion of angelic substance in Book Five is embarrassing but at least it has the virtue of being theoretical. Here his theory is translated into the practical terms of incident, where angelic substance has to be shown in action, flexing its muscles, being wounded, bleeding, and the like. It is bad enough that the angels should be presented as human combatants, and that even their blood should be required to imitate the colour of human blood:

> from the gash
> A stream of Nectarous humor issuing flow'd
> Sanguin. (331-3)

---

[1] *The Works of Samuel Johnson, LL.D.* (London, 1787), ii. 169 ('Life of Milton').

What is worse is that their substance, while simulating flesh, should be endowed with attributes which flesh does not have, and which when applied to it are simply ludicrous:

> The griding sword with discontinuous wound
> Pass'd through him, but th' Ethereal substance clos'd
> Not long divisible.   (329-31)

Apart from the absurdity of the healing process itself (to say nothing of the pedantry of 'discontinuous') it is hardly to be expected that a reader will hang on every word during a battle where the combatants, however grievously wounded, can knit themselves together again without effort. If they can, why should he feel excitement or horror when told that they are 'Down clov'n to the waste' (361) or 'Mangl'd with gastly wounds' (368)? Why should he feel anything at all about them, beyond the fact that they are monstrous curiosities, like green tigers or talking trees?

There are other misjudgements, though few are quite as serious. The speed of Abdiel's first blow is so emphasized as almost to suggest that he struck unfairly (189-93), and the taunting exchange between Michael and Satan (262-95) is much less effective than it was meant to be. Milton wishes to show that Satan's confidence has begun to ebb away, but by qualifying his challenges ('If not to reign') he endows him with something not unlike modesty, beside which Michael's taunts sound strident, very like the 'airie threats' of which Satan accuses him. The section would have been more satisfactory if Satan had replied in the blustering and blasphemous terms given to Moloch (357-60), so that Michael could have seemed comparatively determined, even cool. Then, too, it is strange that angels as yet unfallen should take all night to cast their cannon (492-3, 521-2) when after their fall they build the enormous Pandæmonium in a matter of hours (i. 697). The devils' mining of subterranean minerals from 'Celestial soile', in itself rather unlikely, cannot fail to recall the memorable description in Book One of their excavations in Hell, and Milton's contemptuous dismissal of gold as a 'precious bane' (i. 692), and after this reminder it is awkward, too, to continue with a description of Michael's troops that has them armed in 'Golden Panoplie' (527). Angelic armour is troublesome generally: one wonders why, considering its inconveniences to both sides (595-7, 656-60), it was ever worn. Such responses might be querulous if Milton's grasp on his material were surer. But here they are direct results of the scepticism encouraged by the text, by the incongruities it offers and by the Disney-like panoramas to which it sometimes descends:

> At his command the uprooted Hills retir'd
> Each to his place, they heard his voice and went
> Obsequious, Heav'n his wonted face renewd,
> And with fresh Flourets Hill and Valley smil'd.   (781-4)

Even straightforward and appropriate comments are sometimes tainted by the faults which have preceded them. There is nothing to object to in the picture of Heaven repairing 'Her mural breach' after the expulsion of Satan's army (878-9), except that it is faintly reminiscent of the self-restorations of the wounded angels, and to that extent dubious.

A more general and more serious objection concerns the actual conflict between the armies, or rather the expectations with which the reader is made to come to it, and the inconclusiveness that follows. Milton's approach seems hesitant here, as if he were not quite sure of his purposes, or attempting too much. Certain things suggest that he is anxious to persuade us that the two sides are evenly matched. Evidently realizing that our inclination will be to assume that Michael's army is the stronger, he offers no description of the heavenly forces which can compare with that of Satan's forces in Book One (531-89), and what description he does give is subordinated to the more menacing passages about the rebels (vi. 61-86). This prevents our sympathy from recoiling too easily from the invulnerability of Heaven to the forlorn (and, in romantic terms, therefore splendid) aggressiveness of Satan's army; and a similar control on our responses is maintained by Raphael's use of words like 'ours', 'our', 'us', and 'we' (200, 571,

577, 580), skilfully shifted to 'thir' and 'they' when the heavenly host is involved in a temporary defeat (584-94). Elsewhere, however, this sort of circumspection disappears, and it is fair to say that on the whole we are led to expect that Michael's army will soon prevail. They are described as 'Invincible' (47) and 'irresistible' (65), as 'the Victor Host' (590), and both Abdiel and Michael, whose assessments of the situation one would expect to be shrewd, seem confident that they are about to conquer (116-18, 258-9). Then, too, we learn that some of them have special weapons (320-3) and that unlike the rebels they are 'unobnoxious to be pain'd' when wounded (404), it being suggested that their innocence gives them other more general advantages over their opponents as well (401-3). Every advantage short of a numerical superiority seems to rest with them, and it is natural to expect that they will quickly triumph. Yet in the event they can achieve nothing better than a stalemate. The effect is surely to expose them to our disappointment, to make 'the excellence, the power Which God hath in his mighty Angels plac'd' (657-8) appear equivocal. That Satan's forces should be powerful may be readily conceded, but that they should measure up to Michael's so successfully seems curious. What is more curious is that the whole battle, anticipated with such excitement and described with such attention, should prove to be a fiasco, a sort of sham-fight, as pointless as it is noisy. The account of the aerial bombardment that is the heavenly reply to Satan's artillery is so forceful that we are almost persuaded of the imminence of a heavenly victory; yet scarcely has it begun, the devils joining in 'with jaculation dire' (665), when God intervenes, telling his Son that the contest can never be conclusive (690-4), that 'the Victor Host' can never secure a victory. Milton, it will be said, is leading up to the commissioning and triumph of the Son. That he is doing so is obvious enough; that he is doing so with much skill is not. His disclosure earlier, that

> th' Eternal King Omnipotent
> From his strong hold of Heav'n high over-rul'd
> And limited thir might,   (227-9)

was disconcerting enough, almost sufficient to reduce the conflict
to a controlled and formal display, like a boxing match according to the rules. This is worse: God tells us, clearly and positively,
that as a matter of fact it *is* a kind of boxing match, and one that
can never reach a decision. The effect of such a disclosure, however
belated, is bound to be retrospective. It leaves us wondering what
all the fuss has been about, and why the battle should have been
reported with such fidelity and at such length.

III

What is much more serious, cripplingly serious, is that it leaves
us wondering about God, a crucial figure in the poem to whom
we are already inconveniently hostile. The more one reflects on
it the more devious and dubious does his conduct during the War
appear. There is, to begin with, his original order to Michael,
'drive them out' (vi. 52), an order that is later repeated *verbatim* to
the Son:

> Pursue these sons of Darkness, drive them out
> From all Heav'ns bounds into the utter Deep.   (715-16)

The first order is as categorical as the second and it alone, quite
apart from the word 'irresistible' and the phrase 'the Victor Host',
is enough to make Michael's performance disappointing. Yet, we
are now to understand, it is simply a pretence, a subterfuge. God
knows that 'in perpetual fight they needs must last Endless, and
no solution will be found' (693-4), and that Michael cannot per-
form the task he has been given. In an anthropomorphic God such
behaviour is very nearly as suspicious as it would be in a man. One
can agree that 'Vengeance is his, or whose he sole appoints' (808)
but did he not appoint Michael just as imperatively and officially
as the Son?

The question arises why Michael should be given only half
the troops available, for it is evidently this that ensures the stalemate which follows. At first God seems to imply that no more
than half Heaven's forces are necessary for a victory. That, at least,

is what one would deduce from his orders to Michael (44-55), and
even from his sarcastic remark that they should 'all imploy' in
their defence, 'lest unawares we lose This our high place' (v. 730-
1), a remark which indicates that a numerical superiority over
Satan's legions is quite unnecessary. To confirm this deduction
there are the many suggestions that the rebellious angels are
already, angel for angel, inferior to their loyal compeers: vi. 124-6,
319-23, 394, 401-3, 404-5, 661. Against it we have only God's
assurance that the debilitations of sin have 'wrought Insensibly,
for I suspend thir doom' (691-2), a statement that is so patently at
odds with what is hinted elsewhere that it reads less like informa-
tion than an expression of uneasiness, an attempt to claim impartiality. Yet if he really is impartial why has he bestowed on
Michael a specially tempered sword (320-7), a sword that sets
Satan at an obvious disadvantage in their encounter? Surely such
covert assistance is just as fraudulent as 'the fraud' (555) of Satan's
cannon, a legitimate invention of his own? Why, too, should
circumstance (that is, ultimately, God) permit the rebels to feel
pain when the loyal angels do not? This is not impartiality, but
what is more unsettling is that it is not honest partisanship either.
God's conduct is that of a man who lends his nephew a trowel and
scaffolding to build a house, at the same time making sure that he
will never be able to lay his hands on the right quantity of bricks.
He gives Michael a special sword, and immunity from pain, but
he also withholds from his command the additional 'ten thousand
thousand Saints' (767) who, one must assume, would have enabled
the archangel to conquer.

His purpose in all this is obvious. Whatever advantages
Michael's troops enjoy, and however futile their performance may
seem in view of these advantages, they cannot be allowed to win.
Victory has been pre-empted for the Son, who in due course will
implement the order 'drive them out' and, most impressively, will
do so single-handed. No reasonable reader will maintain that the
Son's assault does not provide a stirring climax to the War, but
what he can maintain, with simple justice, is that God's manner
of proceeding has been unduly shifty, altogether lacking in the

frankness one would expect from him. Why should he find it necessary to hoodwink his own angels? Why should his instructions to them be so precise, so utterly devoid of any qualifications or conditions?

> Go *Michael* of Celestial Armies Prince,
> And thou in Military prowess next
> *Gabriel*, lead forth to Battel these my Sons
> Invincible, lead forth my armed Saints
> By Thousands and by Millions rang'd for fight;
> Equal in number to that Godless crew
> Rebellious, them with Fire and hostile Arms
> Fearless assault, and to the brow of Heav'n
> Pursuing drive them out from God and bliss,
> Into thir place of punishment, the Gulf
> Of *Tartarus*, which ready opens wide
> His fiery *Chaos* to receave thir fall. (44-55)

The speech is surely disingenuous, and the more so for its pretence of frankness. The apparently candid attempt to set up a fair fight between equal numbers, in particular, is underhand and deceitful, for the speaker knows that it is precisely this provision which will prevent the order from being carried out. Later the Son describes God's cause as 'righteous' (804), but if it be agreed that means determine ends this adjective just will not do. God has 'fixed' the fight, much as a crooked boxing promoter might, and he is prepared almost to boast about it to his Son:

> [I] this perverse Commotion governd thus,
> To manifest thee worthiest to be Heir
> Of all things, to be Heir and to be King
> By Sacred Unction, thy deserved right. (706-9)

'None but Thou Can end it', he also says (702-3), implying that this is a matter of fact, beyond his own control. But who has brought it about? Not only has he reduced the heavenly forces to inadequacy, but it is he, too, who transfers upon the Son 'such Vertue and Grace Immense' as can enable him to conquer (703-4). It is all a put-up job, a careful performance to exhibit his Son in the very best light possible. Satan's and Beelzebub's stratagems during the Consult are not more devious.

Our impression that God has misconducted himself is especially unfortunate in view of his decision, which he announces soon after the conclusion of hostilities, to create a new race which will eventually replace the fallen angels:

> But least his heart exalt him in the harme
> Already done, to have dispeopl'd Heav'n
> My damage fondly deem'd, I can repaire
> That detriment, if such it be to lose
> Self-lost, and in a moment will create
> Another World, out of one man a Race
> Of men innumerable, there to dwell,
> Not here, till by degrees of merit rais'd
> They open to themselves at length the way
> Up hither, under long obedience tri'd,
> And Earth be chang'd to Heav'n, and Heav'n to Earth,
> One Kingdom, Joy and Union without end.   (vii. 150-61)

Quite apart from the question whether these lines are perfectly consistent with God's omniscient foreknowledge of the Fall of Man (and surely, as Professor Hughes says, they reveal an intention which overlooks the Fall, and which is frustrated by it),[1] the decision taken in them clearly cannot be what it pretends to be. God is shown undertaking the creation of Earth and Man because a third of the angels have fallen, and this is partly confirmed by Satan at iii. 678-80. Yet elsewhere in the poem we learn that such a creation was contemplated even before the War in Heaven began. In Hell Satan reminds his troops that it was rumoured in Heaven before they were driven out (i. 651), and later he says it had been long foretold (x. 481-2), while Beelzebub speaks of an 'ancient and prophetic fame in Heav'n', and of how God's will in the matter was 'Pronounc'd among the Gods, and by an Oath, That shook Heav'ns whol circumference, confirm'd' (ii. 345-53). We are as ready as ever to allow for the prevarications of these devils—to ask, for example, why a decision so vehemently con-

---

[1] *Paradise Lost*, ed. Merritt Y. Hughes, p. 223 n.

firmed should still be spoken of as a rumour—but even if the widest possible allowance is made God's behaviour is still untrustworthy. If the devils know anything at all about the projected creation then some sort of decision about it *must* have preceded their fall. Why then should God pretend, after their expulsion, that the idea has just occurred to him, as a natural consequence of the depletion Heaven has suffered? Such a pretence is just as dishonest as any lies which can be attributed to Satan or Beelzebub concerning the antiquity of the 'fame' and its confirmation.

Ab actu ad posse valet illatio. We have just been observing God's disingenuous governance of the War, and now we are made to feel that there is something decidedly fishy about his decision to create Man. Inevitably we begin to wonder whether the future Fall of Man will not be similarly 'govern'd', whether it is not simply one more scheme for exhibiting his Son in a very favourable light. It is true that God and Raphael have insisted that Man's will is free, and that God has also pointed out that his divine foreknowledge of the Fall does not imply its predestination. But Raphael is merely God's mouthpiece, not an independent authority, and these assurances would be more convincing if we had not already found God's statements to be unreliable (as his orders to Michael are), if we did not remember the nervous intensity with which in Book Three he tried to persuade us of his utter innocence, and if we had not been told that in the War foreknowledge was very useful to him, permitting him to steer his plan aright:

> And now all Heav'n
> Had gon to wrack, with ruin overspred,
> Had not th' Almightie Father where he sits
> Shrin'd in his Sanctuarie of Heav'n secure,
> Consulting on the sum of things, foreseen
> This tumult, and permitted all, advis'd:
> That his great purpose he might so fulfill,
> To honour his Anointed Son . . . . (vi. 669-76)

Admittedly we are not in a position to declare outright that God's attitude to the Fall is every bit as wily as his attitude to the War.

We lack the criteria to assess his acts of omission, like his allowing Satan to escape from Hell, and we are inhibited from condemning him by the knowledge that in the end, with the Atonement, all will, for virtuous men at least, come right again. But if the clouds of doubt are thick about us they have gathered too about the bright divinity whom the poem set out to justify. We come to the Fall of Man with many reservations and uncertainties. We come to it besides with a willing compassion, not too remote from indignation, for the human victims who must suffer a disgrace incomparably worse than Michael's in the War.

Chapter Five

ADAM AND EVE IN PARADISE

I

DIFFERENT localities in *Paradise Lost* are presented with different degrees of conviction, with the result that some are much easier to imagine than others. Milton's practice shows that this is not primarily a matter of elaboration. The 'windie Sea of Land' (iii. 440) where Satan first alights after traversing Chaos is briefly but memorably described, and it provides as good a preparatory contrast for Paradise as Hell has done. Hell too, though it is more deliberately charted later, is at first a simple design of darkness and fire, and all the more dramatic for its simplicity. Like a diorama's its effectiveness lies mainly in the smouldering blurs of light playing across it. The terrible handicap under which Milton worked, the blindness for which no 'inward' sight could ever truly compensate, since it shut off so much of the raw material of poetry, is almost transformed to an advantage in such descriptions, reduced as they are to bold and broad impressions, where the density given by detail is not needed.

Heaven is much less satisfactory.[1] This is partly because it has, of necessity, so often to be compared to Earth. Where the comparisons involve a perceptible benefit, it is true, they are not troublesome. We can accept the 'Chrystal wall of Heav'n' (vi. 860) for the sake of the Son's exciting expulsion of the rebels, just as, in the story told by a cheerful Jesuit, we can accept a high circular wall in Heaven for the sake of the archangel's reply when questioned about it: 'Those are the Roman Catholics in there. They like to imagine they're alone here.' Where such a *quid*

---

[1] Its very name is abused, being at one time applied to the sky of Hell (ii. 538) and at another used in conflicting senses within a single sentence (ii. 1004-6).

pro quo is lacking, however, the effect is merely 'to set forth Great things by small', and Heaven suffers much the same impoverishment as the anthropomorphism in the poem inflicts on God. Who wants it to exhibit 'Trees . . . and vines' (v. 426-30), or hills, vales, woods, and streams (vi. 69-70), or to be rich in mineral resources (vi. 472-81)? Who wants a Heaven so concrete that after the fall of the angels God has to tell his faithful followers to 'inhabit laxe' (vii. 162), to spread out a bit, so that the vacancies and gaps can go unnoticed? The resort to detail is unnecessarily *gauche*, and it is also contradictory. Heaven is sometimes an orchard-landscape of fruits and vines, but it also seems to be a region of 'thin Aire Above the Clouds' (xii. 74-8); its floor is 'trod'n Gold' (i. 682) but it is also glassy, 'like a Sea of Jasper' (iii. 363, cf. xi. 209); its night is 'grateful Twilight' (v. 645), nothing more, but it brings 'dark' and 'darkness' too (vi. 407, 415); and so on. Applied to Chaos such confusions might be functional; here they are not. Even the splendours of Heaven are partly incongruous. It is true that the task of describing such things, 'inimitable on Earth By Model, or by shading Pencil drawn' (iii. 508-9), is far from easy, true also that the poet's approach to it is sometimes judiciously oblique. The account of Heaven's stairway for example (iii. 510-22), itself 'mysteriously' allusive, is placed just after an account of draughty barrenness, the Paradise of Fools, so that the contrast can heighten a reader's sense of wonder. But the awkward fact remains that the celestial descriptions usually involve materials like 'Diamond and Gold' or 'sparkling orient Gemmes' (iii. 506-7), and that terrestrial opulence of that order is elsewhere contemptuously dismissed as the livery of 'gay Religions' (i. 372), as a 'precious bane' (i. 692), as a sort of gamboge with which imperial servants are 'besmeard' (v. 356), as mere 'dust' on the roads of Heaven (vii. 577), and the like. No one expects a poet to create new elements with which to decorate the structures he imagines in Heaven, but it is reasonable to expect him to avoid decrying materials upon which much of his celestial imagery depends. The expectation is all the stronger when the concord of his Heaven is already liable to be contrasted with the energetic discord elsewhere, in Hell or even Chaos, and to seem merely lethargic in comparison.

Paradise is an easier assignment for poetry because the character of its landscape can be directly described, without constant recourse to analogy. Milton is not afraid of difficulty, however, and perhaps imposes it on himself by telling us that the beauty of Earth is scarcely inferior to Heaven (iii. 552). Whatever the incongruities in his own presentation of Heaven such a remark raises our expectations, and will have to be made good in what succeeds. At first it seems unlikely that it will be. The physical stages of Satan's approach to Paradise are well managed, and our own approach is made through him,[1] but the preparation is less enriching than merely gradual, and to begin with the account of Paradise occasions some disappointment. *Pace* Professor Lewis, and Freud, it is difficult to feel that 'hairie sides' (iv. 135) is a felicitous description of slopes of brushwood, nor is the artificial 'enameld' an adequate epithet for the colours of prelapsarian 'Blossoms and Fruits' (148-9). The 'of pure now purer aire' (153) also, at once appropriate and delicious, is perhaps tainted with sophistication when we read

> now gentle gales
> Fanning thir odoriferous wings dispense
> Native perfumes, and whisper whence they stole
> Those balmie spoiles.
> (156-9)

Other words from time to time intrude some awkward connotations, like the italianism 'Imbround', with its inadvertent suggestion that 'the noontide Bowrs' are dry and sunburned, while the attempt to locate Paradise on a map involves the poet in anachronism:

> *Eden* stretchd her Line
> From *Auran* Eastward to the Royal Towrs
> Of great *Seleucia*, built by *Grecian* Kings,
> Or where the Sons of *Eden* long before
> Dwelt in *Telassar*.
> (210-14)

---

[1] C. S. Lewis, *A Preface to Paradise Lost*, pp. 47-50.

The rills that water the garden (229-30) seem intended to obviate the necessity for anything as disagreeable as rain, but later we hear of 'showers' (646); and later still there appears to be some doubt whether the gates of Paradise are made of ivory or alabaster (544, 778). We also find that Eden can be uncomfortably hot (v. 300-2).

Yet when all the possible objections have been generously allowed for, it remains true that this setting, so vital to the purposes of the poem, is soon as full of enchantment as one could wish. Starting uncertainly, as often elsewhere, Milton seems to gain control as Book Four proceeds, and from about line 236 onwards the verse is almost faultless, and richly evocative. A part of his artistry is reserved, not yet apparent. Only in Book Eleven, for instance, will the position of Paradise on a hill permit some deft ambiguity in the use of phrases like 'nether World' (328) or 'brought down To dwell on eeven ground' (347-8), and its brilliance and colour the desolating force of a splendid seascape:

> Then shall this Mount
> Of Paradise by might of Waves be moovd . . .
> Down the great River to the op'ning Gulf,
> And there take root an Iland salt and bare,
> The haunt of Seales and Orcs, and Sea-mews clang.   (829-35)

Yet already more than enough is evident: a lavishness of language and suggestion seldom surpassed in the entire poem. The glitter and richness of the scene would be outlandish—brooks 'Rowling on Orient Pearl and sands of Gold', trees weeping 'Gumms and Balme' and bearing '*Hesperian* Fables true', flowers consuming 'Nectar'—but it is beautifully clinched by the simplest of phrases: 'and without Thorn the Rose'. One notices too the delicacy with which the scents and sounds of Paradise are fused:

> The Birds thir quire apply; aires, vernal aires,
> Breathing the smell of field and grove, attune
> The trembling leaves, while Universal *Pan*
> Knit with the *Graces* and the *Hours* in dance
> Led on th' Eternal Spring.   (iv. 264-8)

After the mention of birdsong 'aires' are all but 'tunes', but 'vernal aires' brings in the suggestion of scent, and this, after the ambiguous 'Breathing', is at once confirmed by 'the smell of field and grove'. The word 'attune' revives the idea of music, but 'trembling' maintains the counter-suggestion of the 'aires' as 'breezes', so that when the music really emerges, with the 'dance', it keeps the enrichments of scent it has been gathering from phrase to phrase. The technique in lines like these is wonderfully assured, and they are followed by the inspired comparison relating Eden to 'that faire field Of *Enna*', thus in turn relating Eve, prophetic-ally, to Proserpine, 'gatherd' by the ruler of the underworld, bequeathing 'all that pain' to Ceres as to us Eve left her own painful bequest after the Fall. Professor L. C. Knights, in a review of *A Preface to Paradise Lost*, once observed that a fundamental criticism of Milton's Paradise 'is that it is not deeply felt. The inflexible movement, the formal epithets, the often inappropriate imagery betray the lack of that essential quality that Wordsworth called organic sensibility.'[1] The comment is a fair one if we restrict it to the first half of the description Milton provides (131-235), but to extend it to such passages as these would be Draconian. Even when the Proserpine metaphor has passed, and the analogies are scaled back to a more formal level, with encrustations of proper nouns, the undertones in the verse continue faintly but audibly. The '*Nyseian* Ile' and 'Mount *Amara*' (275, 281), for example, are not merely colourful place-names; they denote localities of refuge or retirement, havens of safety, and thus preserve the air of menace that Satan's presence and the reference to 'gloomie *Dis*' have both aroused. Attention is suspended between the beauties of the Garden, 'Chos'n by the sovran Planter' (691) and therefore with justice lavishly presented, and the intruding malice which 'Saw undelighted all delight' (286), a monstrous shadow falling across the grass. Paradise is in fact a far more arresting setting than either Hell or Heaven, for it comprises both the drama of the one place and the celestial beauty of the other.

---

[1] *Scrutiny*, xi (1942), 147.

II

With the entry of Adam and Eve into Satan's view it naturally achieves an even higher degree of interest. Not only have we penetrated to the core of the anthropocentric universe of the poem, and to the two characters upon whom the outcome of the plot depends; we have also established contact, for the first time, with beings of flesh and blood, with people who, despite the obvious qualifications, are very like ourselves. Prototypes they may be, but this in itself gives them a special appeal. Being as yet unfallen they can epitomize those qualities for which we value humanity most, and their appearance can embody all the beauty and grace of which the human form is capable. Its appropriateness is carefully underlined. They are 'Godlike erect' (289), their posture symbolizing their integrity (viii. 257-61); 'The image of thir glorious Maker' shines in them (iv. 291); everything about them radiates the light of a 'Sanctitude' which, though called 'severe' (293), seems gentle and vulnerable, soliciting both our affection and our protectiveness. Perhaps this is partly a result of their nudity, a form of defencelessness that is purged of all associations but the right ones:

> But *Eve*
> Undeckt, save with her self more lovely fair
> Then Wood-Nymph, or the fairest Goddess feign'd
> Of three that in Mount *Ida* naked strove,
> Stood to entertain her guest from Heav'n. (v. 379-83)

One can see, in such a passage, how scrupulously Eve's appearance is safeguarded against the faintest suspicion of immodesty, with the mild 'Undeckt' poised against the more explicit 'nakedness' of the goddesses, itself rather more statuesque (Juno, Minerva) than seductive. Perhaps it is also due to the key-words used in the portrayal of Eve: her 'softness' (iv. 298), as much a matter of ingenuous pliancy as of nubility, her 'Dissheveld' and 'unadorned golden tresses' (305-6), the feature in a woman provoking the most innocent and tutelary of male desires, and her 'coy submission, modest pride, And sweet reluctant amorous delay' (310-11). Then too they are young, with the timeless youth suggested in the chiasmus

> *Adam* the goodliest man of men since borne
> His Sons, the fairest of her Daughters *Eve*　　(323-4)

and, being young, they are also in some degree defenceless, inexperienced. There is something fragile about their innocence and their devotion to each other as they pass 'hand in hand' before our eyes (321), and we are all the more conscious of it because of the baleful presence who stands looking on. In the circumstances it is extremely difficult not to make an involuntary alliance with them, committing ourselves wholeheartedly to their cause.

There is another reason why Adam and Eve appeal to us so strongly. It is because their sexuality is quite untainted, pure and immaculate. This is a matter that deserves to be examined with some care, since it has been very carefully handled by the poet. That certain preparations are made before the subject presents itself is obvious enough: the sexual relationship between Satan and Sin is a 'secret' one (ii. 766), furtive and unsavoury, and as this is the only type of sexuality we encounter before Adam and Eve's theirs naturally tends to seem all the more wholesome, 'sequesterd' and private no doubt (iv. 706) but in no sense surreptitious. Much more important than a preparation of this kind, however, is the quality of inclusiveness that is found in Milton's account of the human pair. Imagine what they would have been like if Tennyson had written Book Four. The beauty, the delicacy, even the charm might all have survived, but it is doubtful whether one would also have come upon two lines like these:

> The savourie pulp they chew, and in the rinde
> Still as they thirsted scoop the brimming stream.　　(335-6)

'They chew', blunt and robust, betrays the presence in Milton of a faculty which is often thought of as un-Miltonic, a faculty which appears again in Book Seven, in that grotesque, naïve, and yet curiously successful picture of the parturitions of Earth:

The grassie Clods now Calv'd, now half appeer'd
The tawnie Lion, pawing to get free
His hinder parts, then springs as broke from Bonds,
And Rampant shakes his Brinded main; the Ounce,
The Libbard, and the Tyger, as the Moale
Rising, the crumbl'd Earth above them threw
In Hillocks; the swift Stag from under ground
Bore up his branching head: &c.   (463-70)

At bottom it is simply an absence of false delicacy, of poetic self-consciousness—the positive side of that tactlessness which is displayed in the matter of angelic substance and diet—and it does much to validate the remoter beauties of Paradise. It does still more to validate the relationship between Adam and Eve, for it persuades us that we are in contact less with paragons, unreal idealizations, than with a man and woman as human as ourselves. The inclusiveness extends particularly to that side of love most often glossed over in elevated modes of writing, and to the flesh through which it operates. We see it later in Adam's frank admission that from the beginning Eve was not 'uninform'd Of nuptial Sanctitie and marriage Rites' (viii. 486-7), but we see it here too, at once, almost as soon as the humans appear:

Nor those mysterious parts were then conceald,
Then was not guiltie shame, dishonest shame
Of natures works, honor dishonorable,
Sin-bred, how have ye troubl'd all mankind
With shews instead, meer shews of seeming pure,
And banisht from mans life his happiest life,
Simplicitie and spotless innocence.   (iv. 312-18)

The intrusion of a personal attitude is actually no more intrusive than the autobiographical exordium to Book Three, and like that it strikes exactly the right note. The effect might almost be called cathartic, an emotional release. Every honest man and woman will admit that sexuality as we know it is a source not only of ecstasy but of self-mistrust. To equate the Fall of Man with the boy or girl's first awareness of this mounting pressure in their bodies, as many do, is merely to indicate, sanely enough, that in this area of human consciousness the imperfections of our nature are especially clear. We are driven by a force with which, because it is natural, we long to be perfectly at ease, but which is also hedged about by doubts and inhibitions. When in art human sexuality is vindicated, when we encounter a representation of desire and fulfilment from which these doubts have been purged off, our reaction is accordingly not so much envy as pure relief. The nostalgia which we all feel for a sexuality that can be perfectly assured, perfectly innocent, instead of a prize to be patiently achieved, is temporarily satisfied, and this in itself is a heartening experience, a reassurance that the prize in fact exists, and is not a delusion. These factors probably account for the gratitude with which, especially in young manhood or womanhood, many readers make their first acquaintance with D. H. Lawrence's novel *Lady Chatterley's Lover*, where sexual fulfilment is presented as a real fulfilment and not as an occasion for remorse or fear. They are reminded that, however imperfect their human condition, they can transcend it, that the chance of freedom is always there. Paradise offers a similar reminder, and our floating gratitude easily attaches itself to the two inhabitants of the Garden, embodiments of an unspoken trust.

The other side, that there is some unsteadiness in the portrayal of Adam and Eve, need not be denied. Their first speeches, like God's and Satan's too, are less than adequate. Adam sounds like a Victorian governess, turning the children's blessings sour with every attempt to count them, and there is even a suggestion of disingenuousness when, having spoken pointedly of death, he has to pretend that the point is a vagary: 'what ere Death is, Som dreadful thing no doubt' (iv. 425-6). The remark is uncomfortably close to Satan's dissembling 'whatever thing Death be' (ix. 695), and it alerts us to those passages in Book Nine (760-4, 826-33, 904 ff., &c.) in which the unfallen pair's knowledge of death seems implausible, as familiar as our own. For her part Eve seems rather a ninny when she accepts what he has been saying as 'just and right' (iv. 443), though fortunately she soon escapes from sententiousness into narrative. One notices also Milton's tendency to attribute to the humans his own views on worship (iv. 736-8, v. 146) and on diet (v. 345), to use occasionally pedantic phrases like 'enormous bliss' (v. 297) in the descriptions associated with them, and to spin out some of their speeches to unnecessary length. Adam at v. 313-20, for instance, almost seems to be persuading a habitually parsimonious Eve to be more liberal in her housekeeping. Yet their credit completely swamps these tiny debits. More important than the iterative imagery of roses, nightingales, and clasped hands that is applied to them, more important than the idyllic existence they enjoy, more important even than their beauty, what draws us to them are the two qualities emphasized at the very beginning of Book Four in the phrase 'innocent frail man' (11). They are less like 'our two first Parents' than like our children, unblemished and defenceless replicas of ourselves, and we feel some of the protectiveness towards them that we feel towards a son and daughter. Above all, they transcend and allay our own troubled longing to break free of the conditions which have made our bodies 'To shame obnoxious, and unseemli- est seen' (ix. 1094). Nowhere is their happiness and innocence more evident than in their sexuality, and this supplies a powerful inducement for us to identify the best of ourselves with them. Do we not seek a sexual adjustment like theirs, 'Founded in Reason, Loyal, Just, and Pure' (iv. 755)? Do we not also repudiate 'loveless, joyless, unindeard, Casual fruition' (766-7)? A word like 'fruition' is emphatically incongruous here. Their relationship is the ideal exemplar of that mutual dependence and comfort to which every human love aspires, the reciprocity of the elm and the vine. While he sustains her,

> she spous'd about him twines
> Her mariageable arms, and with her brings
> Her dowr th' adopted Clusters, to adorn
> His barren leaves.   (v. 216-19)

The impression of warmth and harmony is not inadvertent. Adam and Eve's domestic happiness is to be an important issue in their Fall, and for that reason as much as any the poet has to stress it here, concentrating our view of Paradise until it is sharply focused on their nuptial bower, extolling 'the Rites Mysterious of connubial Love' (742-3), defending the purity of their nakedness and their desire. Inadvertence comes in—if it does—only when this emphasis is persuasive enough to lead us to make common cause with the human pair. That, in any case, is what we do. Whatever degree of idealization their portraits involve it is an idealization of ourselves, of what we know and love. What man, reading the poem, remains perfectly indifferent to the 'meek surrender' of Eve's embraces? What woman can ignore Adam's masculinity, and the gentleness with which he soothes Eve's perturbation after her dream? Their experience is our own, transposed and refined, and it has a far stronger claim on us than the disembodied excellence of Heaven,

III

Surprisingly enough, despite all this, two criticisms of the unflawed felicity of Paradise have been advanced. The first maintains that Adam and Eve's life together before the Fall is idle and purposeless, and consequently unsatisfying to read about. Dr. Tillyard has put it crisply and challengingly, as every critical comment on the poem deserves to be put:

> Reduced to the ridiculous task of working in a garden which produces of its own accord more than they will ever need, Adam and Eve are in the hopeless position of Old Age Pensioners enjoying perpetual youth . . . . We feel that Milton, stranded in his own Paradise, would very soon have eaten the apple on his own responsibility and immediately justified the act in a polemical pamphlet. Any genuine activity would be better than utter stagnation.[1]

The second criticism maintains that even in their prelapsarian state Adam and Eve already show signs of the sinfulness which is to descend upon them later. This, too, has been argued by Tillyard, in his *Studies in Milton*, but the full implications of the view are perhaps most carefully worked out by Miss Millicent Bell. In

---

[1] E. M. W. Tillyard, *Milton* (London, 1946), pp. 282-3.

the interesting essay where this is done she sums the matter up in a single sentence:

> In the poem, the transition from innocence to sin can be felt very early in the narrative—most strikingly in Book IV, where the rehearsal of the temptation presented in Eve's dream already moves her across the border this side of innocence, and Book VIII, where Adam in conversation with Raphael reveals that thus early Eve's influence over his judgment is no longer compatible with a state of innocence.[1]

That both criticisms are serious hardly needs pointing out. If Adam and Eve's existence in Eden seems futile then clearly to identify ourselves with them is much more difficult than has been claimed. Worse, if they have the appearance of fallen creatures even before their Fall then this is bound to confer on them some of the dubiety and shiftiness that surrounds God during the War in Heaven. Are such impressions justified by the poem? The curious fact about criticisms of Adam and Eve, unlike those of God, is that they often turn out to be unreal, conceivably justified by subsequent and abstract reflexion but certainly not by the impact of the poetry as we read it. These two sound plausible, but the possibility must be faced that they are also of that kind.

Consider the first of them. There can be no question of hard labour in Paradise if it is to deserve its name, and the most one can expect is that Adam and Eve should be sufficiently busy to prevent the reader from thinking of them as lotos-eaters. This, surely, is precisely what the first allusion to their mild employments in the Garden ensures:

> They sat them down, and after no more toil
> Of thir sweet Gardning labour then suffic'd
> To recommend coole *Zephyr*, and made ease
> More easie, wholsom thirst and appetite
> More grateful, to thir Supper Fruits they fell.   (iv. 327-31)

To expect real effort and real exhaustion in such circumstances is rather like expecting a golfer to dig a sizable dam with his niblick, not by accident, after the cartoonist's fashion, but in a deliberate

---

[1] 'The Fallacy of the Fall in *Paradise Lost*', *P.M.L.A.* lxviii (1953), 867.

agony of exertion. Labour in Paradise, Milton makes clear, is really a diversion, a 'delightful task' (437). In a sense it is unnecessary, since the produce of the Garden requires no augmentation; but it is seemly that Adam and Eve's gratitude should express itself in the desire 'To prune these growing Plants, and tend these Flours' (438), and understandable that they should want to safeguard the delights of leisure by eschewing them for part of each day. Another passage is worth quoting:

> To morrow ere fresh Morning streak the East
> With first approach of light, we must be ris'n,
> And at our pleasant labour, to reform
> Yon flourie Arbors, yonder Allies green,
> Our walk at noon, with branches overgrown,
> That mock our scant manuring, and require
> More hands then ours to lop thir wanton growth:
> Those Blossoms also, and those dropping Gumms,
> That lie bestrowne unsightly and unsmooth,
> Ask riddance, if we mean to tread with ease.   (623-32)

Adam's 'must' does not imply external compulsion, the necessity that obliges a farmer to feed his family and his labourers; it is a gardener's 'must', marking the incentive they both feel to keep their home attractive, neat and trim. And that, in a garden, is as much as can be reasonably expected. Being the persons they are they naturally take their employment seriously, and it is quite right that they should. There is much to do:

> What we by day
> Lop overgrown, or prune, or prop, or bind,
> One night or two with wanton growth derides
> Tending to wilde.   (ix. 209-12)

The verse itself is sometimes used to suggest how much there is that awaits their attention every morning. Observe how skilfully the relatives 'how' and 'what' are organized in this passage to convey an impression of variety:

> Awake, the morning shines, and the fresh field
> Calls us, we lose the prime, to mark how spring

> Our tended Plants, how blows the Citron Grove,
> What drops the Myrrhe, and what the balmie Reed,
> How Nature paints her colours, how the Bee
> Sits on the Bloom extracting liquid sweet.   (v. 20-5)

It is a variety of the senses that will hardly tax them, but after the mention of their 'Plants', and of 'drops' and 'Bloom' ('Those Blossoms also, and those dropping Gumms . . . Ask riddance'), it contributes indirectly to other passages where their work is described. Paradise is a prolific riot of scents and colours, with flowers 'Powrd forth profuse on Hill and Dale and Plaine' (iv. 243), and they owe it to God to keep it from disorder. It is in this sense that they speak of it, gratefully and truthfully, as 'this delicious place For us too large' (729-30).

One additional point about the human pair's activity in the Garden ought not to be overlooked. When Adam says 'Man hath his daily work of body or mind Appointed' (618-19) he reminds us that exertion need not be exclusively physical, and this in turn should remind us that much of their time, like that of children, is spent in discovery, in learning what to think and how to behave. Saint Gregory Nazianzen suggests that God made Adam 'a husbandman of immortal plants' not only literally, but in the sense that he was also the curator 'of Divine conceptions, both the more simple and the more perfect',[1] and a rather similar suggestion is implicit in Milton's account of Adam and Eve, whose activities in Eden go well beyond the limits of manual labour. Time and again they are seen questioning, probing, extending the comprehension they already have. Eve questions Adam about the moon and stars (iv. 657-8), while Adam asks many questions of Raphael, their heavenly guest. We feel, and are meant to feel, that much of the attraction which Satan's temptation has for Eve lies in its promise of enlightenment, of the 'Wisdom' and 'Knowledge' to which he repeatedly refers. Admittedly on that occasion her curiosity goes too far, but that does not mean that the acquisition of legitimate knowledge is not

---

[1] 'The Second Oration on Easter' (*Oratio* xlv), § 8: φυτῶν ἀθανάτων γεωργὸν, Θείων ἐννοιῶν ἴσως, τῶν τε ἁπλουστέρων καὶ τῶν τελεωτέρων.

an important part of their existence. Because we see them acquiring it, as also because we see them planning and executing the management of their unruly estate, any suspicion we may have that they are idle soon disappears. Their occupations may be idyllic and unexacting, but they are real ones too, and shown to be real.

So much for their labour, but what about their innocence? For the moment I shall confine myself to the question whether Eve's dream can be reasonably adduced as a sign of sin. The artistic function served by the dream is not, of course, in question. Everyone will agree that Milton put it in to bridge a possible gap between Book Four and Book Nine, and everyone will also agree that it achieves this object completely. As their prayer just afterwards (v. 166-204), with its allusions to the bounties God has provided, prepares for the account of the Creation in Book Seven, so the dream itself anticipates the events of Book Nine, at some points touching on the very phrases used there. When Eve says that 'damp horror chil'd [her] At such bold words voucht with a deed so bold' (v. 65-6), or mentions 'the pleasant savourie smell' of the fruit (84), the proleptic references to certain lines in Book Nine (740-1, 890, 921) cannot be missed. But does this mean that she is already tainted with the infirmity which her disobedience will bring? The point is again worth examining with some care.

The first account of the dream deals with Satan's activity in brief and general terms. Ithuriel and Zephon find him

> Squat like a Toad, close to the eare of *Eve*;
> Assaying by his Devilish art to reach
> The Organs of her Fancie, and with them forge
> Illusions as he list, Phantasms and Dreams,
> Or if, inspiring venom, he might taint
> Th' animal Spirits that from pure blood arise
> Like gentle breaths from Rivers pure, thence raise
> At least distemperd, discontented thoughts,
> Vaine hopes, vaine aimes, inordinate desires
> Blown up with high conceits ingendring pride. (iv. 800-9)

Two processes can be distinguished here, and neither implies the slightest corruption in Eve herself. If Satan uses 'The Organs of her Fancie' to create the dream he uses them as a material, not a co-operative agency. She is a passive or neutral instrument through which he works to secure his end, no more. If on the other hand he succeeds in tainting her 'animal Spirits' that is not because they are already tainted. It is because his 'art' is powerful enough to force its way into her body, like an infection, disturbing the innate harmony that exists there. Her 'discontented thoughts' are not her own, but have been temporarily induced in her by the force of Satan's will. The qualification 'temporarily' must not be forgotten. When the baneful influence is withdrawn she is herself again, though naturally troubled by the memory of what has been intruded into her mind.

There is little to disturb such an interpretation in the more detailed account of the dream in Book Five, unless one chooses to misconstrue the device which Milton employs to make Satan's suggestions sound unusually persuasive. The speech of the 'gentle voice' which Eve reports to Adam admittedly begins by faintly echoing her own and Adam's remarks on the previous evening (iv. 657-8, 674-6), and it is possible that the blind poet had forgotten that these were not overheard by Satan, who took himself off at iv. 536. But even if Eve's own mind is partly involved in the dream during this initial stage there is no reason to suppose that the involvement continues. As Adam says,

> Som such resemblances methinks I find
> Of our last Eevnings talk, in this thy dream,
> But with addition strange.   (v. 114-16)

It is the addition which is evil, and Eve herself is aware that it is unlike a normal dream, which arises solely in the mind of the dreamer (v. 31-5). Here, as in the brief account quoted from Book Four, the agency working upon her is represented as external: 'methought Close at mine ear one call'd me forth' (35-6). Significantly, too, it is only by assuming a disguise, as with Uriel in Book Three and Eve herself again in Book Nine, that

Satan is able to penetrate even her unconscious defences: of the voice that speaks to her she tells Adam 'I thought it thine' (37). Once Satan has reached the organs of her fancy the external agency disappears, so that she dreams in her own person (48-53), but even then her condition is trance-like, her experience vicarious and induced. Satan reappears in a different disguise, and this time he echoes not her words but his own (60-1, cf. iv. 515-17), in due course hypnotizing her dreaming mind into believing that she cannot do otherwise than taste the fruit (86). Soon afterwards she awakes, her relief at recovering control over her consciousness plainly implying its subjugation during the dream:

> O how glad I wak'd
> To find this but a dream!   (92-3)

It is perhaps clumsy that exclusively Eve-elements, so to call them, should be introduced in the first stages of the dream, but their importance need not be exaggerated. Milton seems to be trying to anticipate the technique which Satan will employ during the temptation proper—the rehearsal of Eve's own thoughts, combined with flattery, followed by an insidious extension of those thoughts—and in any case he later takes care to assure the reader, through Adam, that Eve's innocence survives intact once the wicked influence is withdrawn:

> Evil into the mind of God or Man
> May come and go, so unapprov'd, and leave
> No spot or blame behind.   (117-19)

The point has already been established that beauty is not compatible with inner corruption (iv. 835-40) so that Eve's beauty, too, is meant to warrant her sinless state. Her appearance during the dream strikes Adam as feverish, but its loveliness remains intact: 'Beautie, which whether waking or asleep, Shot forth peculiar Graces' (14-15). Like Adam, she is as 'innocent' as ever (209), having been 'Created pure' (100). There are other dreams in the epic to confirm such an interpretation, for they also depend on an external agency for their content: Adam's in Book Eight, which suddenly 'stood' at his head (292), and Eve's later dream in Book Twelve, in which God advises her of the future awaiting mankind (610-14). In neither of these cases would anyone contend that the dream reflected the subliminal intent of the dreamer. Why then should Eve be suspect in the other case?

A subsidiary argument Miss Bell puts forward, that Eve's admiration for her own reflection (iv. 461-7) betrays a quality of 'dainty vanity' in her, seems equally fallacious, at any rate if we are to give to 'vanity' a tone of incipient reproof, as her context suggests we should.[1] The incident is actually one of the most engaging glimpses we have of Eve's artless simplicity, much like Adam's self-discovery at viii. 267-9, and the childlike honesty with which she compares the physical appearances of Adam and herself is wholly disarming (iv. 477-80). But this is only one instance of the many revelations Milton gives of her charm or femininity. One notices also the humility which leads her to suppose that she can never make Adam as happy as he has made her (iv. 444-8), the modesty that moves her to postpone for a little their nuptial rites by drawing out the 'gentle purpose' of their conversation (641-58), and the conscientiousness of her housekeeping, especially when a heavenly visitor is expected (v. 331-49). One last passage is worth quoting at length, for its delicate suggestion of her maternity, for its sympathetic insight into feminine psychology, and (as will be seen later) for the bearing it has on her eventual Fall:

> So spake our Sire, and by his count'nance seemd
> Entring on studious thoughts abstruse, which *Eve*
> Perceiving where she sat retir'd in sight,
> With lowliness Majestic from her seat,
> And Grace that won who saw to wish her stay,
> Rose, and went forth among her Fruits and Flours,
> To visit how they prosper'd, bud and bloom,
> Her Nurserie; they at her coming sprung
> And toucht by her fair tendance gladlier grew.
> Yet went she not, as not with such discourse

Delighted, or not capable her eare
Of what was high: such pleasure she reserv'd,
Adam relating, she sole Auditress;
Her Husband the Relater she preferr'd
Before the Angel, and of him to ask
Chose rather; hee, she knew would intermix
Grateful digressions, and solve high dispute
With conjugal Caresses . . . .   (viii. 39-56)

The one fault here, and indeed the one fault in Milton's handling of
Eve throughout the central books, is that her withdrawal from
the company is apparently overdue. It is awkward and impolite
of Raphael to say to Adam 'warne Thy weaker' (vi. 908-9) if she
is still present at that point, and indeed her silence had led us to
suppose that she withdrew at some unspecified point in Book
Five. Moreover, she later remarks that she 'over-heard' the
departing angel's words about Satan (ix. 273-8), which would seem
to refer to viii. 633-43 (where, however, Satan is not mentioned)
and to imply that she did not hear his earlier warning at vi. 900-12.
Yet at vii. 50-1 she is listening attentively to Raphael's narrative,
and only in the passage quoted does she actually rise and take her
leave. Milton has deliberately soft-pedalled her presence during
the angel's admonitions, so as to make her unsuspecting pliancy
in Book Nine more plausible, but there is surely some mis-
management in the means he uses. Taciturnities are as useful to a
poet as words are, but they ought not to be misleading.

IV

Nothing has been said so far of the charge which Miss Bell
brings against Adam, that in Book Eight 'Eve's influence over his
judgment is no longer compatible with a state of innocence',
because this raises problems which deserve to be considered
separately. It is unfair to isolate the exchange between Adam and
Raphael upon which it is based (viii. 521-94) and to draw inferences from that alone. What one should do is to trace the relationship that develops between Adam and the angel during their long

conversation, examining the concluding exchange between them in the light of this relationship. To attempt this is to realize that polarization by human contact, as I have called it, is again at work. The phrase may seem unsatisfactory, begging the question whether the polarization concerned is taking place in Milton's mind or the reader's, and perhaps obscuring the point that the one process might be quite independent of the other. But to speak of minds at all, rather than artistic problems, is usually unnecessary, not to say hazardous, and I believe the point at issue can be stated more generally and in more tangible terms.

I have tried to indicate that a real disparity exists in the presentation of the various figures who appear in *Paradise Lost*. The disparity is there in the text, so that it can reasonably be called objective, and its presence can be accounted for without extravagant conjecture about Milton's preconscious mind. God and the heavenly angels are not inadequate because of an illicit and unacknowledged hatred in the poet, but simply because, as an artist, he cannot completely project his feelings into the unsubstantial mould that their existences provide. Satan is at first more sympathetically realized, not because Milton secretly admired wickedness, but because the mould that is offered will admit of more projection, incorporeal identity in this case approximating more to the familiarities of human nature. But the scope that Adam and Eve provide is altogether wider and more inviting. There is very little in them to check the flow and fullness of the poet's imagination or his sympathy, which can accordingly reach out to plumb their every thought and mood. After all, it is not as though they are specific individuals, whom it might be possible to hold at arm's length. They are prototypes, generalizations. Whoever touches them touches mankind, Milton and ourselves included. Though ultimately a product of 'mind' the disparity alluded to is accordingly due less to intention than to the plasticity of the artist's materials, the opportunities which are afforded him by the different characters he is describing. Only two of these characters seem to invite more speculative conjectures: the Son of God, and the Michael of the final books. Both are celestial spirits, which would lead one to expect that their presentation would be as defective as Gabriel's or Raphael's; yet in point of fact both are handled with some of the insight and delicacy found in the portraits of Adam and Eve. Why? I see no other way of accounting for this than by supposing that their quasi-human status has freed Milton's imagination from the inhibitions which the other celestial personages induce. The Son is a potentially human being, and it is easy for Milton to endow him with the authority and gentleness of the incarnate Jesus, to extrapolate from his historical behaviour a suitable character for his disincarnate essence. The procedure would seem to be entirely natural, and perhaps necessary too: how else could a poet go about to comprehend a Being so elusive? Michael again, though his identity is less surely comprehended, is demonstrably superior to his fellow-angels, and it seems reasonable to attribute this to his comparatively human status, as was suggested earlier. In both cases some degree of conjecture about Milton's unconscious processes seems permissible. With the other personages in the poem, however, it is otiose: their presentation depends less on Milton's involuntary predilections than on their tractability as raw material for his poem. For this reason the phrase that has been used, polarization by human contact, is justifiably neutral. In one sense the polarization may be thought of as occurring in both the poet's and the reader's mind; in another it should be thought of as inhering in the dramatic situations themselves, in the conditions of poetic composition under which any poet attempting what Milton attempts would be obliged to work.

The results are easiest to trace when human and spiritual beings are simultaneously present, as Adam and Raphael are during Books Five, Seven, and Eight. Anyone can see how natural and charming Adam's impulses and reactions are made to seem. Observe the courtesy of his assumption that Raphael must be as hot as he is himself (v. 369-70), a courtesy that is all the more engaging because it is misguided. Consider the disarming modesty with which, when Raphael has patronizingly alluded to the limitations in human nature (503-5), he accepts the angel's patronage. Observe how naïvely he attributes to the sun, the stars, and to Sleep itself his own enthralled attentiveness to Raphael's words (vii. 98-108), bestowing on the angel that most absolute of compliments, one which is innocent of flattery. Every word, every response, serves only to confirm the impression we have of his humility and friendliness, and inevitably our admiration for his interlocutor, sensed as more of a monitor than a friend, begins to falter. There is the diffidence of Adam's inquiry concerning Creation (vii. 80-97) and, set against it, the guarded tone of Raphael's reply: 'This also thy request with caution askt Obtaine' (111-12). There is Raphael's moralized and rather incoherent account of the cosmos (viii. 66-178), with its typical admonitions to 'be lowlie wise' (173), and, set against it, the generous politeness of Adam's reply: 'How fully hast thou satisfi'd mee, pure Intelligence of Heav'n, Angel serene' (180-1). There is Adam's spontaneous gratitude to God for his existence too (viii. 278-82), a disposition that is all the more attractive in view of Raphael's ponderous insistence that it is necessary (v. 501-3; vii. 631-2; viii. 170-2). The contrasts between them are almost imperceptible, or would be if Raphael were isolated, an unattached individual; but he is not. He stands as the representative of that heavenly polity around which nebulous prejudices have been steadily gathering, and this means that his deficiencies are much more likely to be exaggerated than ignored. It is not a question of Milton's unconscious mistrust of angels. It is simply that the surge of his imagination, reaching out to embrace the human figure, eddies and hesitates in the face of an identity as remote from his experience as the angel's is. In consequence, while Adam's manner is warm and instinctive, the angel's seems comparatively chilly, too strange and too deliberate to be other than uninviting. Raphael betrays the grudging austerity so often sensed in the personages of Heaven, in Uriel (iii. 696-8) and in God himself (iv. 467), and our sympathy is deflected upon his nominal inferior.

The reader's response to the final interchange between the man and the angel, so conditioned, is much less straightforward than might be assumed. Adam's praises of Eve provide the basis for their remarks and must be given:

> When I approach
> Her loveliness, so absolute she seems
> And in her self compleat, so well to know
> Her own, that what she wills to do or say,
> Seems wisest, vertuousest, discreetest, best;
> All higher knowledge in her presence falls
> Degraded, Wisdom in discourse with her
> Looses discount'nanc't, and like folly shewes;
> Authority and Reason on her waite,
> As one intended first, not after made
> Occasionally; and to consummate all,
> Greatness of mind and nobleness thir seat
> Build in her loveliest, and create an awe
> About her, as a guard Angelic plac't.   (viii. 546-59)

To a strict and judicial mind this will seem very nearly impious; to minds as indulgently disposed as ours have become, however, it is inoffensively hyperbolical and no more. The first few lines are important here, for while their content is perfectly innocuous the repeated 'seems' which makes it so tends to be tacitly carried over into what follows, 'falls' being read as 'seems to fall' (551), 'Looses' as 'seems to loose' (553), and so on. Nor is this reading wilful and unwarranted, as will appear if we glance at a later speech of Adam's to Eve herself:

> I from the influence of thy looks receave
> Access in every Vertue, in thy sight
> More wise, more watchful, stronger, if need were
> Of outward strength.   (ix. 309-12)

Despite their prospective irony these lines present a juster account of the influence Adam receives from his wife and, realizing this, we see too that the key to his statements to Raphael is that they are metaphorical. It is what the intrusive 'seems' has already sufficiently conveyed, what our instinct has already detected, for if we look again at the terms of his praise we see at once how emotional they are, how his love has suddenly burst through his equanimity into imperfect expression. Does he honestly believe that 'All higher knowledge in her presence falls Degraded'? The answer is clearly that he does not, that this is merely a periphrastic way of reporting the intensity of his devotion, for everything we have seen of their relationship belies the statement. It might be argued that later higher knowledge *will* fall degraded; but even that is a contention which, as we shall see, the poem itself does little to support. Certainly for the present there is no evidence to substantiate Adam's words, and we accordingly accept them more for their implications than for their literal meaning.

Raphael, however, does not. According to his lights his response may be the correct one, but there can be no doubt that with his reproofs and his 'contracted brow' (560) he forfeits a further share of our regard. What aggravates the position is that he goes on to speak slightingly of human passion, a subject still charged for the reader with the magical force of the hymn to wedded love in Book Four. Consider the angel's persuasiveness here:

> But if the sense of touch whereby mankind
> Is propagated seem such dear delight
> Beyond all other, think the same voutsaf't
> To Cattel and each Beast; which would not be
> To them made common and divulg'd, if aught
> Therein enjoy'd were worthy to subdue
> The Soule of Man, or passion in him move.   (579-85)

It is a crude attempt to reduce the physical relations of men and women to animality, the last clause descending to plain nonsense, and there must be few readers who do not at once repudiate it, preferring Milton's earlier celebration of this 'dear delight'. Adam himself, to his credit, is only 'half abash't' (595), and gently suggests that 'the genial Bed' of marriage deserves a much more sensitive appraisal, an attitude of 'mysterious reverence' (598-9). Who will disagree with *him*? Even the more acceptable points in Raphael's speech stir up our opposition, partly because of his chilly insistence on the 'rational' and 'judicious' quality of love (587, 591), but mainly because we dispute his authority to discuss the subject at all. We question his experience of any love like Adam's, or our own, and are unimpressed by his blushing evasions (618 ff.) when Adam asks him whether spirits also love. Even if they do, we realize that their love is only another curiosity, as remote from ours as are their modes of digestion. The effect is to reduce his injunction to 'weigh with her thy self; Then value' (570-1) to the same level as his implicit invitation to mount 'the scale By which to heav'nly Love thou maist ascend' (591-2): neither course seems to have much to recommend it. The core of the angel's advice to Adam can be put in four words, 'Love God before Eve', but the whole force of the poem supplies the firm retort, 'Who would?' The real centre of attention is steadily shifting from God to Man, and it is significant that in the exordium to Book Nine Milton should turn from the justifiability of Heaven's decisions to claim that human suffering and steadfastness, 'the better fortitude Of Patience and Heroic Martyrdom' (31-2), are especially suitable subjects for 'Heroic Song'. The poetic material he has to handle, now recalcitrant, now much more amenable, is modifying his interests and allegiances, and our own responses are involved in radical adjustments too. The real test for a reader's sympathies comes with the Fall of Man itself, and it is to that event that we may now proceed.

Chapter Six

THE FALL

BOOK Nine is the longest and unquestionably the most important in the poem, pseudo-questions about the hero and the climax notwithstanding, and since Milton's artistry is also at its best here the book deserves particular attention. Comparison with Vondel's account of the Fall of Man, as in the case of the War in Heaven, soon reveals a sharp discrepancy between the poets' performances, but this time the comparison is all in Milton's favour. In *Adam in Ballingschap* the need for compression has forced the dramatist to leave far too much to his actors, and only their efforts can save the temptation from seeming perfunctory and unlikely. Adam excuses himself from Eve's presence; Belial appears and asks her to grant him the single favour (*loutre gunst*) of eating the apple; and after he has given a rather hurried account of the deific effect of the fruit (1162-72) she obligingly does so. In *Paradise Lost* there is scope for a much more gradual and persuasive treatment, which Milton is brilliantly successful in supplying. The interest of the poem, which has flagged during the preceding books, mounts steadily as Book Nine proceeds, not of course because we are in doubt about the outcome but because we are curious as to how it will be managed. It is, too, a richer and fuller interest that is found here. Much of the writing displays the qualities which would normally be expected from a great novelist or dramatist rather than a poet: a firm grasp on the character of the protagonists, a faultless ear for the intonations each would use, and a profound insight into their moods and motives. Yet interspersed between the speeches, in which these qualities are clearest, there are passages where the appeal is eminently poetic, a matter of linguistic intensity, of colour and connotation and cadence, and these contribute immeasurably to the fascination of the book as a whole.

Two results of Milton's approach may be briefly noted. First, because it is nicely adjusted to the mobility of its changing subjects the epic style seems much less ponderous here. Despite Professor Lewis's widely accepted classification of *Paradise Lost* as a secondary epic it seems preferable to regard it as tertiary, far more remote from an oral tradition than Vergil ever was,[1] and it is arguable that in such a production special attention needs to be given to the poetic texture or surface in order to avoid monotony. Even in Book One—a remarkable artistic achievement and one that is enriched and diversified by many epic similes—this desideratum is to some extent neglected, the narrative devices being frequently indistinguishable from those used in the dialogue:

> Say first, for Heav'n hides nothing from thy view
> Nor the deep Tract of Hell, say first what cause
> Mov'd our Grand Parents in that happy State,
> Favour'd of Heav'n so highly, to fall off . . .? (27-30)

The pattern of rhetorical question, parenthesis, anaphora, hyperbaton, and other oratorical figures, evenly sustained through narrative and dialogue alike, evokes a sense of sameness which, prolonged through the succeeding books, permits the reader's attention to slacken. For too much of the time the verse seems mannered and unresponsive, and even when a speech is said to be made 'in haste' its speed is only a shade faster than the sober norm (iv. 561-75). In Book Nine on the other hand, where the interest might almost be called alternately poetic and dramatic, continually shifting between the vividness of the descriptions and the nuances of the speeches, there is more than enough to keep our attention lively and sharp. This result is pure gain, and seems to be one that the poet has consciously courted. The second result of his approach is probably inadvertent, and although it adds much to the appeal of the book it is not really in harmony with his ostensible purpose. Because his comprehension of his characters is so acute and sympathetic, like that of a novelist, their behaviour

---

[1] *A Preface to Paradise Lost*, pp. 39-60.

seldom seems simply wrong, and there are some striking opportunities for applying the maxim *tout comprendre, c'est tout pardonner*. The effect, as will appear as our analysis proceeds, is to set the human protagonists in a much more favourable light than would seem to be advisable, bearing in mind the declared intention of the poem.

I

The account of the temptation, like the poem itself, begins with Satan who, some little time after Raphael's departure (63-7),[1] has returned to Paradise either 'wrapt in mist' (75, 158) or in the form of one (*Argument*, 180), it is not clear which. Milton does very interesting things with time in *Paradise Lost*, keeping to a tight chronological sequence while at the same time contriving to suggest that the action is spread over several months, but at this point we are barely conscious of the interval, so that the temptation will have to be thoroughly persuasive if Eve's surrender is not to seem impulsive or contrived. Satan's mood, one of *après moi le déluge*, is at once established as recklessly spiteful—

> now improv'd
> In meditated fraud and malice, bent
> On mans destruction, maugre what might hap
> Of heavier on himself   (54-7)

—and even when he adduces two belated motives for his spite (143-57) they seem unconvincing, as though he were merely trying

---

[1] Rajan computes this period as a week (*Paradise Lost and the Seventeenth Century Reader*, p. 68), which raises very perplexing problems regarding Satan's course and ground speed after leaving 'the Equinoctial Line' (64). A better interpretation would be to take 'continu'd Nights' (63) as 12-hour periods, his whole journey consisting of eight of these in the arrangement 3 + 4 + 1 (four days and four nights in all), but this in turn requires 'circl'd' (65) to have the rather strained meaning of 'half-circled', and probably means thinking of the equinoctial and solstitial colures as meridians as well. In view of the uncertainty of the season ('Eternal Spring'!), of Satan's velocity, and of such terms as 'continu'd Nights', 'circl'd', 'Carr of Night', 'traversing', and even 'Colure', to say nothing of the poet's reliance on both Ptolemaic and Copernican cosmology, these five lines may fairly be called the most impenetrable in the twelve books of the poem.

to rationalize the unreasoning malevolence he has suddenly un-
covered in himself. This is subtle and convincing. Now that he is
on the brink of another overt act of defiance he is unmanned by
the subconscious thought that God is hardly likely to let it go
unpunished, and this induces a neurasthenic intensity in him, a
vindictiveness or ferocity that is all the more powerful because he
cannot explain it to himself. The skill with which Milton conveys
'the hateful siege Of Contraries' in his mind can be seen in his
soliloquy, where two verbal reminiscences are aptly employed to
suggest it. 'Rocks, Dens, and Caves' (118) fleetingly recalls the
pointless variety of Hell (ii. 621) and the mood of frustration or
futility associated with it; while 'all good to me becomes Bane'
(122-3) half-echoes 'all Good to me is lost; Evil be thou my Good'
(iv. 109-10), an utterance which was as full of resolution as this is
full of petulance and uncertainty. Obliged to admit that he
cannot hope to profit from the task he has undertaken (126-8)
Satan tries to fix his mind on the eminence to which his acts
will entitle him—

> To mee shall be the glorie sole among
> The infernal Powers, in one day to have marr'd
> What he *Almightie* styl'd, six Nights and Days
> Continu'd making   (135-8)

—but it is clear that this is only a half-hearted attempt to distract
himself, to suppress the fear already divulged in his statement,
'though thereby worse to me redound' (128). An inveterate actor,
but one who has previously reserved his performances for others,
he is here engaged in acting to himself, a point that is well
brought out when he goes on to speak doubtfully of God's
creation of the angels: 'if they at least Are his Created' (146-7).
This was the argument he offered to his followers before the War
in Heaven (v. 853-63), and that it was a pretence his own words
in an earlier book made plain: 'whom he created what I was'
(iv. 43). Now, alone, he offers it to himself, revealing a new capacity for self-deception, and he proceeds to invent such reasons as he
can for his irrational rebelliousness (150-7).

That Milton is working here much as a dramatist would can be inferred from the whole speech, which is as close to stage soliloquy as anything in the poem, not excepting the soliloquy on Mount Niphates, where fragments of 'Adam Unparadis'd' are thought to lurk. It is interesting, therefore to observe Satan pausing to explain his actions and intentions, unnecessarily, but exactly as a character in a play might do:

> Of these the vigilance
> I dread, and to elude, thus wrapt in mist
> Of midnight vapor glide obscure, and prie
> In every Bush and Brake, where hap may finde
> The Serpent sleeping, in whose mazie foulds
> To hide me, and the dark intent I bring.   (157-62)

That could be from *Comus*. It is as though, essaying a dramatic speech, the poet had included even the dispensable accidents of such writing. An obvious advantage offered by this departure from the stylized idiom often employed in other speeches is that it permits more abrupt transitions, and Milton makes good use of them to show the fluctuations in Satan's feelings. The indignation of 'O foul descent!' (163) changes to a despairing sense of futility with 'Revenge, at first though sweet, Bitter ere long back on it self recoiles' (171-2), and that in turn at once veers off into the recklessness we have already detected in him: 'Let it; I reck not, so it light well aim'd' (173). He gives the impression less of thinking than of whistling to keep his courage up, and his last sentence is clearly meant to show how crude and fanatical his mental processes have become: 'spite then with spite is best repaid' (178). This is exactly like Moloch's proposals to pay God back in his own coin (ii. 63-70) and, like Moloch's, it hardly impresses us as a rational and deliberated plan.

A single deficiency may be noted, though it is one which only gradually emerges. It concerns Satan's responsibility for the acts of the creature whose form he enters just after his soliloquy, a question that is handled with unnecessary clumsiness. In Milton's favour it must be admitted that in the Book of Genesis (3 : 14-15) the serpent is specifically condemned for its part in the Fall of Man: a text so positive a man of his convictions would be understandably reluctant to ignore. Still, in the very different context of the poem, to condemn the serpent for the deeds which it performs unwittingly, under Satan's control, is grossly unfair. A clear distinction is needed between the reptile and the spirit who has usurped its form; and it is also necessary to shade the biblical account towards metaphor, so as to avoid attributing unjust behaviour to the Son of God. In many passages this is precisely what Milton does. Satan speaks of 'us' (ix. 475) as though the serpent and he were two distinct identities; he is said to use the 'Serpent Tongue Organic, or impulse of vocal Air' in conversation (529-30), which approximates his acts of speech to those of a ventriloquist; and the Son of God himself admits that 'Conviction to the Serpent none belongs' (x. 84). It is possible, too, that the *New English Dictionary* is mistaken, and that when Milton applies the word 'Inmate' to Satan while he is hidden in the serpent (ix. 495) it is used in its older sense of 'lodger' (cf. Donne, 'The Anniversarie', line 18) rather than the modern sense. Again, the following lines are plainly concerned to reinterpret the literal meaning of the biblical account:

> Yet God at last
> To Satan first in sin his doom apply'd,
> Though in mysterious terms, judg'd as then best. (x. 171-3)

Elsewhere, however, the distinction between the devil and the form he has chosen is smudged over (iv. 349; ix. 188-90, 633-4; x. 494-9, 517), and at one point Milton makes the astounding claim that the Son's condemnation of the serpent was perfectly justified:

> To Judgement he proceeded on th' accus'd
> Serpent though brute, unable to transferre
> The Guilt on him who made him instrument
> Of mischief, and polluted from the end
> Of his Creation; justly then accurst,
> As vitiated in Nature. (x. 164-9)

Granted Professor Hughes's observation that 'unable' here refers to the serpent, not the Son, and granted that the passage is hastily qualified by the lines already quoted, the argument remains wholly unacceptable, and should either have been excised or carefully rewritten. To condemn the serpent 'justly' for Satan's acts is to hold Eve responsible for the substance of her dream, to convict guns of murder and matches of arson. The sequence of events becomes shrouded in a mist of doubt through which we again discern, dimly, the arbitrary conduct of a representative of Heaven. What makes it all the more serious is that the Son has seemed, so far, to be the one celestial figure upon whose honesty we could unhesitatingly rely.

Satan's preliminary movements being accounted for, attention shifts to those of Adam and Eve. They come forth from their bower and, having prayed, begin to plan their labour for the day, 'for much thir work outgrew The hands dispatch of two Gardning so wide' (202-3). The tasks confronting them are rightly stressed, for it is Eve's awareness of them that leads her now, in accordance with the practicality we have already glimpsed in her nature (v. 331-49), to propose that they should work apart. The proposal is entirely natural and clearly dictated by the least frivolous side of her character: together, she feels, they will waste time in 'Casual discourse', whereas apart much can be done. To condemn her for making it would be to fall into the fallacy of *post hoc, ergo propter hoc*, and few readers apart from Miss Bell are likely to do so.[1] Adam gives her due credit for her suggestion, though perhaps his tone is a little priggish (231-4), but he makes the mistake of claiming, as his first argument against it, that there is no demand upon them for 'irksom toile' (242). Eve is experiencing that very common mood when in prospect a task seems unusually daunting, and Adam's reasoned circumspections, all but slothful to someone feeling as she does, are hardly likely to allay it. A stint of hard work will. His first objection accordingly gets them off on the wrong foot altogether, and when he goes on to say that they will be safer

---

[1] See *P.M.L.A.* lxviii (1953), 870.

in one another's company, obviously meaning that she will be safer in his (251-2, 265-6), she is understandably ready to prolong the discussion. What endears her to us is that she does so 'With sweet austeer composure' (272), gently and equably. Surely, she asks (285-9), Adam does not feel doubtful about her ability to stand alone?

The honest answer would be 'Yes, I'm afraid I do' but one can sympathize with Adam's reluctance to return it. In his embarrassment he first suggests that they should 'avoid Th' attempt it self, intended by our Foe' (294-5), advice which is sound enough, though impracticable, but he continues by claiming that even an unsuccessful temptation 'asperses The tempted with dishonour foul' (296-7), an argument which is nonsensical and which Eve is quick to controvert (331-6). He recovers himself sufficiently to point out, shrewdly, that their enemy must needs be subtle, 'who could seduce Angels' (307-8), but blunders again when he asks 'Why shouldst not thou . . . thy trial choose With me, best witness of thy Vertue tri'd' (315-17), not seeing, as she does, that the trial is then no trial at all. Eve demurs, of course, but modestly and 'with accent sweet' (321). Troubled by the weakness of his arguments and the ease with which she disposes of them he is then obliged to admit quite frankly that she is right, that he is afraid she may be weak, or at least deceived. He softens the aspersion by claiming that it is not mistrust 'but tender love' which prompts him to make it, but his observation that, by 'Not keeping strictest watch', her mind may be misled (359-63) reveals that this is not quite true. Recovering himself again he shifts to the firmer ground of an admonition, 'Trial will come unsought' (366), but spoils this by arguing that a witness is necessary before her resistance to temptation can be attested (368-9). The remark is improvised and unconvincing: obviously if she reported to him that she had met and worsted the tempter Adam would not demand a judicial inquiry. And at this point his objections collapse: he gives his consent to her departure. Far from being sudden, the decision is almost inevitable, two causes having conspired to bring it about. First, he is unnerved by the thought which has just struck him, that their trial will come when it is least expected. If this is so then Eve may as well go off at once, while she is freshly warned and on her mettle. Secondly, his wife's gentle persistence has forced him to acknowledge, to her and to himself, that her complaint at 285-9 is justified. He feels guilty for mistrusting her, and tries to make up for it by letting her have her way. So, claiming the last word, though 'yet submiss' (377), she withdraws her hand from his and takes her leave.

What is so remarkable about this conference is that neither Eve nor Adam has forfeited one jot of our regard during its course. Their speeches are once again in the epic manner, leisurely and deliberate, but the manner is functional now, and allows the discussion to go forward in a way that is perfectly amicable, devoid of all heat or contentiousness. Then, too, because their points of view are only gradually brought out there is ample opportunity for us to identify ourselves now with one and now with the other of the disputants, to feel our way into their minds with insight and understanding. Any suggestion of abruptness, as with the Adam of Vondel's play, or of obstinacy and irritation, has been scrupulously avoided. Moreover, Milton sees to it that both speakers should have a proper claim on our attention by giving them the kind of views which plainly deserve to be heard. True, we are aware of the irony when Eve says that she does not 'expect A Foe so proud will first the weaker seek' (382-3), and when they agree to meet again at noon with 'all things in best order' (402), the latter as irony which the poet takes pains to underline (404-11). But granted her basic premise that she will not fall, a premise which is at this stage as nearly justified as it possibly can be, Eve has reason on her side in every statement that she makes, and it is quite impossible to regard her as thoughtless or foolhardy. To read her speeches is to become convinced, for the moment, that she will not fall, for every point she advances is lucid and persuasive—a fact which greatly enhances the demureness of her replies. Adam's rejoinders are deliberately made to seem inferior so that this advantage will remain with her. Yet if she may be said to hold the aces of reason he in turn undoubtedly holds the trumps of intuition, and our knowledge that he will in the event be proved correct obliges us to listen just as attentively to his stumbling and uncertain warnings as we do to Eve's quiet good sense, to share his feelings just as fully as we find ourselves sharing hers. The most accurate paraphrase for our response to their conversation is thus almost a paradox: both are right, but Adam is righter because events will prove him so. It is a response which the contrast between their honesty and Satan's tortuous self-delusions helps to confirm. There we could watch an irrational mind entangled in its own pretences; here we see only candour and innocence. Apart from the relationship between Satan and the serpent, a difficulty which in any case only emerges later, the first four hundred lines of the book, a crucial prologue, could hardly be better managed.

II

Eve is alone and busy with her flowers, providing for them the support she herself now lacks, when 'to his wish, Beyond his hope' Satan encounters her (421-33). Here we observe how, the psychological interest briefly receding, poetry flows in to take its place. The scene is vivid with floral colours, 'Carnation, Purple, Azure, or spect with Gold' (429), and the freshness that Eve personifies as she stands among them is admirably caught in the simile that compares her to a country virgin, like the milkmaid of contemporary literature an embodiment of innocent comeliness (445-54). For a few moments Milton allows us to feel the force of beauty and virtue emanating from her, a radiance that disarms the devil himself, who pauses to watch her in forgetful admiration, 'Stupidly good' (465). But scarcely has the tableau of simplicity and malice counterpoised been glimpsed than it stirs into dramatic life. Satan reminds himself of the ugly satisfaction to be got from finding her 'Thus earlie, thus alone', and of the formidable task ahead, and he comes surging towards her with the unnatural writhings of the prelapsarian serpent, the grace of his movements as sinister and unsettling as Eve's has been captivating. So, moving 'With tract oblique' (510), he works his way forward until 'Hee

I

boulder now, uncall'd before her stood' (523). As in the early stages of her dream the agency of temptation is external and extraneous. We await its entry into her consciousness.

Satan's first speech to her is precipitate in comparison with the recent exchanges between Adam and herself, a sudden plunge into flattery the momentum of which carries him importunately forward to his suggestion that she should think herself 'A Goddess' (547), and Milton's first comment, 'Into the Heart of *Eve* his words made way' (550), is regrettably premature. As often before, the poet begins unsteadily and it seems that for the moment his subject is eluding him. With Eve's reply, however, he takes command of it and the unsteadiness departs. Quite naturally, but with an unintentional evasiveness that allows the devil's flattery to stand unchallenged, she expresses her astonishment at hearing a 'Tongue of Brute' uttering 'human sense' (554). It is a miracle, she feels, and she is understandably eager to hear it repeated:

> Redouble then this miracle, and say,
> How cam'st thou speakable of mute, and how
> To me so friendly grown above the rest
> Of brutal kind, that daily are in sight?
> Say, for such wonder claims attention due.   (562-6)

'Speakable' is clumsy, and was in 1667, but there is nothing else to object to here. Milton has made skilful use of the speech to remind us of two vital points which our anticipations had already contrived to blur. First, we remember that Satan is still 'Meer Serpent in appearance' (413) and consequently no fit object for suspicion or alarm. As late as ix. 905 the identity of the tempter is 'yet unknown' to his victims, and not until x. 1032-5 does Adam connect the serpent's deceit with Satan. From Eve's point of view, then, the reptile's unexpected articulacy is a 'wonder' only, that and no more. Wonders enough have been crowded into her short life and this latest example is less exceptional than it might seem. Secondly, in accordance with her unsuspecting curiosity her innocence is again exhibited, an innocence that is close to charity here. For surely it is charity, even more than surprise, which leads her to accept the serpent's flattery for what she presumes is the 'friendly' intention behind it, instead of denouncing him for speaking intemperately? The other interpretation, that she is actually gratified, is much more difficult to swallow. For one thing, Milton's bald assertion that 'Into the Heart of *Eve* his words made way' has already predisposed us to defend her, if necessary against the poet himself. For another, Satan's compliments have been so sudden, and so extravagant, that we are at a loss to imagine the Eve we have come to know accepting them as valid praise. A little later, for instance, she will be seen reproving the snake for 'overpraising' the magical tree, and at a time when she is sharply conscious of its possible virtue (615). Simply because her modesty and wit have been so amply demonstrated we take her words to show her sensitiveness, her unwillingness to hurt the feelings even of a snake, and one whose words might easily be taken as an affront, a caricature of compliment. Whatever the poet's intention her integrity accordingly still appears quite unflawed, and her gentleness is even more evident than it has been. Yet her curiosity about the serpent's ability to speak has left an opening for persuasion, and it is through this that Satan is able to proceed.

He speaks more cautiously this time—'Empress of this fair World' she is, though not 'A Goddess'—but with a hyperbolic undertone that is carried over from his salutation (568-70). He is cautious too in explaining how he came to eat the fruit which has loosened his tongue. Careful to leave the 'goodly Tree' on which it grew unspecified, he is equally careful to suggest that his behaviour was representative, a mere translation into action of the wishes of his fellow-animals:

> Round the Tree
> All other Beasts that saw, with like desire
> Longing and envying stood, but could not reach. (591-3)

By far the most important passage in his speech, however, is that in which he briefly outlines the intellectual powers which the fruit conferred:

> Thenceforth to Speculations high or deep
> I turnd my thoughts, and with capacious mind
> Considerd all things visible in Heav'n,
> Or Earth, or Middle, all things fair and good.   (602-5)

The oblique reminder of Raphael and Adam's discussion of cosmology in Book Eight which Milton introduces is no accident, and it gives sudden power and cogency to Satan's words. Remembering Eve's departure from the company, and what was said on that occasion concerning the pleasure she takes in speculative discussions with her husband (viii. 39-56), remembering, too, her intellectual inferiority to Adam (iv. 297-8), we see at once how impressed she must be by this report, and can easily infer the questions that are stirring in her mind. If she were to eat the serpent's fruit would not her own mental powers suffer an equivalent expansion? And if that happened would not her conversations with Adam be even more satisfying than they already are? Thus, disturbingly, temptation begins to pass into her consciousness where, since it feeds on her own desires and hopes, it can spread and intensify. The chance is offered her, apparently, to be a better and more companionable wife than she has so far been, to replace Raphael himself, whose conversation has so enthralled her husband. The wish is as innocent as ever, but clearly dangerous, and the element of danger makes the scepticism of her next remark equivocal:

> Serpent, thy overpraising leaves in doubt
> The vertue of that Fruit, in thee first prov'd:
> But say, where grows the Tree, from hence how far?   (615-7)

Such a response is typical of her lucidity and moderation, but it is also a challenge to the serpent to make good his claim. She is inviting him, not merely to lead her to the fruit, but to prove its efficacy too, if necessary upon herself. Hers is exactly the sort of mistrust with which we greet exciting but unconfirmed good news. Not daring to believe that his report is accurate, and misled by his deliberately vague account of the tree's position (627-30), she tells the serpent to lead the way.

There is much to admire in what comes next. The resort to a short excursion at this point, so that the temptation can fall into two stages, one remote and one immediate, is itself a stroke of genius; and it is matched by the simile which, a more heightened kind of utterance again returning, Milton uses to body forth the implications of Eve's progress towards the tree. Here the actual and the metaphoric terms of the simile are wonderfully aligned: Satan with an 'evil Spirit' indirectly perceived, temptation with 'Boggs and Mires', and Eve herself with an 'amaz'd Night-wanderer' unwittingly led into mortal danger. No sooner is the poetry lifted to this pitch of intensity than the psychological interest, in turn, usurps its place. Recognizing the tree, Eve feels her hopes collapse. Yet her curiosity lingers, betraying itself in the scepticism with which she once more questions the properties of the fruit:

> . . . The credit of whose vertue rest with thee,
> Wondrous indeed, if cause of such effects.　　(649-50)

Again the faint note of challenge can be detected, and again the impulse of her heart can be inferred. So closely are her own interests involved, so strong has her desire to improve her companionship now become, that she finds herself hoping against hope that some kind of dispensation will be found, to permit her to eat and, having eaten, to enjoy the liberating powers the fruit can bring. Immersed in her own feelings, preoccupied, she speaks flatly and unenthusiastically of the prohibition and of the liberty they otherwise enjoy, her very tone an invitation to the serpent to pursue the subject, to find the dispensation that she wants:

> God so commanded, and left that Command
> Sole Daughter of his voice; the rest, we live
> Law to our selves, our Reason is our Law.　　(652-4)

Even a stupid tempter would perceive some kind of opportunity here, and Satan is far from stupid, as his next question shows. Is the fruit 'Of all these Garden Trees' prohibited then? Unwary Eve, still speaking tonelessly, with none of her former animation, still preoccupied with her disappointment, replies that only the one tree has been forbidden (659-63). And now, just as he intended,

Satan's chance has come, the chance to pose the specious question 'Why?', to play upon the dissatisfaction which he can see working in her. Minutely sensitive to her mood and therefore 'more bold' again (664), collecting himself like a Demosthenes or Cicero, he launches into a passionate speech to vindicate her wishes.

It is characteristic that even at this most critical moment he should still retain the orator's sense of address, of the appropriate tricks and tactics, and that he should begin by speaking directly to the tree. Momentarily ignored, Eve is put at a psychological disadvantage, and her attention is also diverted to the fruit on the branches, apparently so innocuous and inconsequential. In reading (cf. 735-7) one has the impression that her eyes remain fixed on the tree while the serpent's voice alternately rings and purrs in her ears—a trance-like state which, recalling her dream, makes her Fall seem all the more plausible. Her attention thus caught, Satan applies himself to dispelling the first of her fears, the fear of death. The serpent has not died; why then should she? Indeed he has found a 'life more perfet' than he ever knew before (689). Proceeding, he appeals to her spirit, to whatever sense of adventure she possesses. Surely even God will approve of intrepidity, the ability to risk and win?

> Shall that be shut to Man, which to the Beast
> Is open? or will God incense his ire
> For such a petty Trespass, and not praise
> Rather your dauntless vertue, whom the pain
> Of Death denounc't, whatever thing Death be,
> Deterrd not from atchieving what might leade
> To happier life, knowledge of Good and Evil;
> Of good, how just? of evil, if what is evil
> Be real, why not known, since easier shunnd?
> God therefore cannot hurt ye, and be just;
> Not just, not God; not feard then, nor obeyd:
> Your feare it self of Death removes the feare.   (691-702)

So far as it goes, the logic is superbly tight. Forget the one argument that he suppresses, that they must not eat because to do so is to disobey, and what he urges is not only persuasive; it is to all intents and purposes true. And immediately he turns from the negatives of refutation to the sonorous positives of persuasion, assuring her of the benefits that must follow if she will eat, the reiterated 'Gods . . . Gods . . . Gods' running like an incantation through his speech. Under its spell the reader becomes one with Eve, understanding that she is scarcely conscious of argument any longer, of reason or consequence. Satan's comparisons, his blasphemies, his questions—all seem to blur in the haze of her own desire, in what he now correctly describes as her 'need' of the fruit (731). We can sense how her mind is closing as the surge of surrender flows over her, dark and warm, that voluptuous and vertiginous abandon which James Joyce has called 'the swoon of sin'. Himself also sensing it, with a tact that is fearful Satan falls silent.

Milton is less than fair to his own artistry when he maintains, after this, that Satan's words have won 'too easie entrance' into Eve's heart (734). If the entrance is easy it is only because the persuasion has been consummately framed, and all but irresistible. To have followed it intently is to know that by this stage the moment of decision has already passed, though without being fixed and pointed. Whether Eve knows it or not she is committed to disobedience, and will eat the fruit. This imparts to the self-communing speech which follows a curious unreality, as if in the interests of irrationality she were trying somehow to recover her rational grasp on her feelings, and even on the hunger which she is now experiencing (740), to explain to herself what excuses might be advanced for the course she is going to follow. It is almost pathetic to see how, with a parenthetic 'doubtless' (745), she tries to recapture the scepticism of her earlier remarks, ambiguously, nevertheless at once brushing the hesitation aside with the phrase 'too long forborn' (747), a clear indication that she has accepted most of the serpent's logic. Actually her reasoning in the body of her speech (758-68) is simply a repetition of Satan's, a more or less formal rehearsal of the arguments in favour of transgression, and it is only towards the end that her own independent intelligence seems to assert itself. The word 'envie', for instance, which Satan has tentatively applied to God (729), has penetrated her trance, but she applies it to the serpent who, having tasted, 'envies not, but brings with joy The good befall'n him' (770-1). She is not overtly rebellious, as Satan has very nearly disclosed himself to be, but is trying rather to rationalize the determination that has suddenly filled her. Independently too, perhaps, she makes the additional point that the prohibition is unfair, itself preventing her from assessing the issues which it involves:

> What fear I then, rather what know to feare
> Under this ignorance of good and Evil,
> Of God or Death, of Law or Penaltie?   (773-5)

Yet all her arguments, whether her own or derived from Satan, are somehow irrelevant, the mere reflexes of a usually incisive mind now borne along on a flood of emotion. Here, to hand, is the pledge of domestic felicity, 'the Cure of all' (776), the enchanted food that will guarantee, once and for all, her full equality with Adam. More, it will perhaps even make her superior to him. The idea has monopolized her whole being, and it is with her imagination fixed on the endless perspectives of happiness which it promises that she stretches her hand out and plucks the fruit.

III

So compressed an account of Eve's Fall cannot hope to reflect the richness and subtlety of its original, and a further objection to it might be that compression has rendered it far more lenient than accounts of this section usually are. But surely it is precisely the quality of lenience which brings it closer to one's actual experience in reading, for the whole force of the poem up to this point is such as to dispose a reader to lenience. One of the commonest faults in Miltonic criticism is to wrench the characters and incidents of *Paradise Lost* from their artistic context, and then to consider them either as if they were autonomous or as if they were simple copies of their doctrinal or traditional equivalents, disregarding the significance which has been conferred upon them by the poem. Professor Lewis's Satan is an unusually persuasive example of this tendency, but Professor Douglas Bush's God shows clearly just how dangerous it can be. By dint of quoting from Hooker and the Cambridge Platonists Bush is able to establish something like a seventeenth-century conception of the Deity, but the figure that emerges bears about as much relation to the God of Milton's epic as the historical Macbeth does to the hero of Shakespeare's play.[1] Many orthodox commentaries on the events of Book Nine seem almost equally misdirected. Their consistency is with Milton's *obiter dicta*, like 'that foul revolt' (i. 33), or with Christian belief in general, rather than with the preceding two thirds of the poem. No truly critical account can afford such infidelity, for it must reckon not only with the text of Book Nine itself but equally with the conditioning factors working upon the reader as he reads it. To dismiss Eve as a delinquent, and little more, is to violate the artistic integrity of the poem as a whole.

This is not to pretend that she is guiltless. Analysis of the text so far has suggested that there are two chief inducements which lead to her surrender—her wish to be an ideal companion, and her wish to put on the quality of a goddess—and the second of these is quite as reprehensible as the first is praiseworthy. Her conduct after she has eaten the apple, too, is described in such a way as to make its unrighteousness perfectly plain. Even as she is eating she falls into the sin of gluttony, devouring the fruit 'Greedily . . . without restraint' (791), and she has hardly finished before she is promising to visit the tree 'Not without Song, each Morning, and due praise' (800), just as if her morning prayers are henceforth to be offered to it rather than to God. So, too, a strain of rebelliousness, excluded from her speech as late as 770, where she declined to attribute envy to God, now comes filtering into what she says, in her sly and cryptic reference to the envy which 'others' feel about the fruit (805) and in her characterization of God as 'Our great Forbidder' (815); while the wisdom on which she so prides

---

[1] *Paradise Lost in Our Time* (Ithaca, 1945), pp. 40-4, 68-9.

herself is exposed as sheer folly when she persuades herself that perhaps God has not noticed her transgression (811-16). Worst of all, on an ethical if not a theological level, is the selfishness which comes to the surface as soon as she considers whether or not to share the fruit with Adam. All thought of his welfare is swept from her mind, and it is only to keep him from 'another *Eve*', for herself, that she decides to implicate him (826-31). Finally, lest any doubt as to her guilt should still remain, she is shown bowing in homage to the 'power' in the tree, which is simply her own disobedience hypostatized and deified (835-8). It would seem that the signs of her infamy could hardly be more conspicuous.

Still, to brand her as infamous requires an effort, and one which the reader is encouraged to neglect. Nor is this simply because his sympathy, estranged from her immediate adversary, Satan, and her remoter adversary, God, has no one else but her upon whom it can fix itself. The position is more complex and more interesting. In the first place, although her aspiration to 'God-head' is a vicious one, in itself quite indefensible, the process by which she has arrived at it is not. Her initial motive for interesting herself in the fruit was the wish to improve her intellectual powers, and thus to qualify herself as an adequate substitute even for Raphael in her husband's eyes. As she now in effect confesses, it was

> to add what wants
> In Femal Sex, the more to draw his Love,
> And render me more equal, and perhaps,
> A thing not undesireable, somtime
> Superior. (821-5)

However impugnable on strictly moral grounds such a motive is hardly likely to move a reader to condemn her; and at the same time he can see how comparatively easy it was, under the hypnotic persuasion of Satan's speeches, for the motive to enlarge beyond its proper limits, transforming itself into a more general desire for 'knowledge' as such, the attribute of 'the Gods who all things know' (804). Merely to grasp these motives is to go part of the way towards excusing her decision to eat the fruit: *tout comprendre*, *c'est tout pardonner*. In the second place, despite the gravity of her misdemeanours, they all, except for her gluttonous ingorging, take place after she has eaten, by which time it is easy for a reader to feel that he is no longer in contact with the true and essential Eve. Just as her mind is usurped and dominated by the force of Satan's will during her dream, so here one is persuaded that the fruit itself is determining her behaviour, like some hypnogenetic and noxious drug. She is 'hight'nd as with Wine' (793)—as we say, 'under the influence'—and although this is not a complete defence to the indictment which can be brought against her it makes her conduct much less intolerable than it would otherwise have been. Thus even at this stage she still retains some sort of hold, precarious but tenacious, upon our sympathies.

What about Adam meanwhile? So preoccupied has the reader been with Eve that the reappearance of her husband provides a perceptible shock, a poignant reminder that all her actions must now be reviewed from a different angle—his. The shock is allowed to linger during the lines which follow, for in them the wretched disparity between his expectations and the brute facts of the occasion is carefully emphasized. The garland of flowers he has woven to crown her, 'As Reapers oft are wont thir Harvest Queen' (842), recalls the pastoral innocence which cloaked her when Satan first intruded upon her solitude, and his eagerness for her return harks back to his earlier saying that 'short retirement urges sweet returne' (250). Such reminiscences heighten the dramatic tension as he comes to meet her: it is almost as though the two worlds, of innocence and disaster, are about to collide. In a way that any ordinarily superstitious reader can readily understand Adam has been troubled, working for the first time in the strangeness of isolation, by a fitful presentiment that all may not be well with her (845-6). Or possibly this is one of those telepathic links which so often spring into being between a husband and wife. He can scarcely be prepared, however, for the tale she has to tell him.

She tells it with a strange blend of innocence and dishonesty. As Professor Hanford has acutely observed, the 'stage imagery' introduced at this point ('in her face excuse Came Prologue, and Apologie to prompt') at once suggests that she is acting a part,[1] and when she tells Adam that she has missed him and found time hanging heavily (857) it is plain that she is lying too. Like the serpent earlier she is careful to insinuate the normality of what she has done, in this case by immediately pointing out that the serpent ate before she did (867-71), and she extenuates her guilt still farther by claiming that she has only 'tasted' the forbidden fruit (874). Most disagreeable of all is her pretence that she has sinned for Adam's sake, not in the sense that she wanted to make sure of his love, which would be the truth, but because she wanted to make him truly happy (877-85). Yet in all this darkness of lies and evasions some faint glints of her former innocence can still be detected. Behind her promise never to work apart again (859-61) one can sense her unspoken promise, as pathetic as it is futile, never to fall again; behind her statement 'which for thee Chiefly I sought' (877-8) there moves the shadow of the truth which it might have had; behind the 'distemper' which flushes her cheeks (887) there lies a mind well aware of its guilt and duplicity, and already ashamed of them. She is corrupt, selfish, dishonest—all the accusations usually heaped upon her by the commentators— but she retains some of her prelapsarian identity also, enough to be the object more of a horrified compassion than of plain disgust.

Next comes what Waldock called 'the crisis of the poem', the Fall of Adam, an episode analyzed by him with such brilliance and finality that it hardly needs extensive comment here. Put very briefly, the conclusion at which he arrives is that Adam's Fall is due entirely to his love for Eve, that he falls 'through love as human beings know it at its best, through true love',[2] and that only by a submission to inhumanity or rigid preconceptions can the reader condemn his behaviour. This is one of those critical *aperçus* which has the absoluteness that a fact has, and can never be undermined. Far from being romantic, or sentimental, it is the

---

[1] *The Poems of John Milton* (2nd edn., New York, 1953), p. 414 n.
[2] *Paradise Lost and Its Critics*, p. 52.

one interpretation which a truly hard-headed scrutiny of the text confirms; and the consequences are just as Waldock says. Adam can rightly adduce 'The Bond of Nature' as the basis for his decision (956)—for him not to fall would be in every sense unnatural—and only by inverting our own natures and values can we even begin to reproach him. His Fall in consequence, far from seeming a defection, must strike us as a necessary and courageous sacrifice.

An important point to notice is that the decision is, or appears to be, virtually instantaneous, unhesitating. Like those 'Acts of God' which, Raphael has said, while being 'Immediate . . ., more swift Then time or motion', still require the 'process of speech' to describe them (vii. 176-9), Adam's 'inward' speech at 896-916 seems more like the spatial elaboration of a single moment than a normal soliloquy. This flexibility or artifice in the use of dialogue can be seen elsewhere in the epic, for example in Adam and Eve's simultaneous delivery of a long speech in Book Five (153-208; and cf. iv. 724-35), where we accept the lines for their content and are distracted from imagining two voices speaking in awkward unison. The pity is that Milton did not somehow contrive to introduce it into Satan's first speech in Book One also, a speech which, as was noted earlier, is all too clearly a conventional address, and therefore very nearly grotesque. Another important point to notice is that the true reason for Adam's decision is the first one that he gives:

> How can I live without thee, how forgoe
> Thy sweet Converse and Love so dearly joyn'd,
> To live again in these wilde Woods forlorn? &c. (908-16)

He will fall because he loves her. Though other reasons are suggested in the speech which follows, addressed not to himself but to Eve, they are really only afterthoughts put in to minimize her anxiety: just as he did after her dream, Adam is trying to comfort her. He does so immediately and accidentally, as it happens, by calling her 'adventrous' (921)—a remark which presumably reminds her of the serpent's claim that God himself will respect her courage (693-7)—but the inadvertence soon gives way to conscious intention as he goes on to echo her own arguments, surmising that to follow the serpent is less heinous than to lead the way (927-32), and that the fruit must surely make them 'Gods, or Angels Demi-Gods' (937). Specious the arguments may be, but their effect is almost as moving as it is ominous here. Even in the jaws of death, poised ready for his tremendous plunge, itself the pledge of his devotion, Adam can pause to speak gently to his wife, cheering her spirits with whatever reassurances he can find.

Love then, the highest degree of human love as we know it, is now the focus of attention, and Adam and Eve's speeches emphasize its power. They do more: they vindicate the force of love as an exalted and ennobling one. Adam's devotion to his wife can fairly be called magnificent, and we should be less than human if we did not admire and honour him for it. Nor ought we to forget that Eve herself does so, for it is because she does that one can speak of his love as ennobling. He may be urged on to disaster by it, but its effect on her is clearly to refine and strengthen her corrupted soul. What is her reaction when she hears that he has resolved to fall with her?

> O glorious trial of exceeding Love,
> Illustrious evidence, example high!
> Ingaging me to emulate, but short
> Of thy perfection, how shall I attaine . . .   (961-4)

Prior to this one might have said that Adam's utter fidelity put her selfishness to shame. But here she shows that she has realized this herself, and that the realization is sweeping aside the disloyalty and egotism bred in her by the fruit. Traces of pettiness, perhaps more endearingly human than contemptible, still remain in what she says, as when she hopes aloud that their 'one Crime' may yet not be a crime (971-2), or persuades herself that the fruit is 'good' (973). But she has realized what a momentous experience it is that they are sharing, and her state of mind is one in which it is more and more difficult for pettiness to survive. Reversing the selfish position she had taken she tells Adam that she would willingly die for him, now that she is assured of his 'so true, So faithful Love unequald' (977-83), and it is impossible not to believe that she means it, that the words have come welling up from the fullness of her heart. Her character, until this moment arrested in its own completeness, has suddenly begun to develop, to comprehend a deeper level of experience than it has so far known.

In more general terms the same is true of their love. Idyllic and perfect it has been; now, forgoing perfection, it reaches out after maturity. The change is a matter of loss as well as gain, but it is the gain which seems most striking.

> Our State cannot be severd, we are one,
> One Flesh; to loose thee were to loose my self.   (958-9)

Put these lines into the mouth of the Adam of Book Four and they are the conventional protest of a lover, heartfelt but un-inspiring. Return them to their context in Book Nine and they become heroic, an agonized promise to follow Eve into the desolation to come. Backed as it now is by momentous issues, by a sense of tragedy and disaster, their love takes on a much deeper resonance than it has had before. And Milton reminds us that this is partly their own doing, that Adam is deliberately throwing his happiness away. His mind is 'not deceav'd, But fondly overcome with Femal charm' (998-9). Waldock objects to the words as a judgement, and an unfair one, on the motives involved, but if the ambiguity in 'fondly' can be admitted they seem quite masterly. Adam falls 'fondly'—foolishly, lovingly. And we fall with him, sharing his generous improvidence, trusting his love.

IV

The immediate sequel, presented in the last two hundred lines of the book, can be most expeditiously dealt with by reducing it to three stages: lust, concealment, and dissension. Of these the second is probably the least significant. Milton uses it effectively enough to show the new self-consciousness which the Fall has aroused in Adam and Eve (1091-8) and to suggest, perceptively, that the real wish underlying their actions is to hide the transgression itself (1113-14, 1119-20); but there is comparatively little here to fix or modify our attitude towards them, which now depends upon more weighty considerations than their nakedness. Much more important is their declension to lewdness and quarrelling, for such lapses are bound to affect a reader's attitude. The question is to what extent they do so. Let us take the two stages in the order in which they occur in the poem.

There are two principal reasons why the lust of Adam and Eve after their Fall should seem less repulsive than Milton apparently intended, less of a clear-cut contrast with their innocent relations in Book Four. The first and most obvious is that the fruit which they have eaten is frankly admitted to be an aphrodisiac, 'Carnal desire enflaming' (1011-13). No doubt if they had deliberately eaten it in order to heighten their desires the position would be different; as things are, however, its 'operation' is something which they could hardly be expected to foresee. Some commentators, it is true, would prefer to hold them responsible for all the consequences of their disobedience, even as unpredictable a consequence as this. But in criticism, as in Law, one's standard must be the standard of a reasonable man, not an inquisitor or a bigot, and such a standard cannot be invoked to condemn them here. Like Eve's a little earlier their conduct is induced and almost involuntary, and this fact by itself is nearly enough to excuse it. The second reason, less simple but almost equally extenuating, is suggested when Milton calls their acts 'The solace of thir sin' (1044). If it is an unconventional reason that is because it goes deeper than convention, to the core of our real feelings. The unconventional truth, after all, is that lust can be largely divorced from depravity—can be simply a matter of uncomprehending acquisitiveness, misguided but understandable, an attempt to objectify and capture the elusive quality we call love. This again is especially true at a time of crisis, when love and life are both hanging in the balance. The idea provided the basis for a brief interlude in a film which came out some years ago, *Lifeboat*, from a scenario by John Steinbeck. Just as the lifeboat is apparently foundering, its timbers awash, the patrician newspaperwoman and the labour organizer with whom she is at loggerheads clutch at each other in an abandoned embrace, all sense of decorum gone, overbalancing into the water between the thwarts. The scene was effective because it was honest and true. Under the threat of imminent death a man or woman's natural modesty is easily displaced by the craving to snatch some kind of trophy from life while it lasts, and it is common knowledge how this craving can take the form of an imperious sexual hunger. Such a reaction is not so much lustful as possessive, the uncontrollable impulse to seize and comprehend a principle of life before life itself is snatched away. The human spirit, like a guttering lamp, affirms itself in a dying flare.

Now surely if we are ready to look a little below the surface (as we should be) this is not so very remote from Adam and Eve's embraces at this juncture in the poem? Every reader regrets the corruption of that innocence which was so attractive in Book Four, but it has served its ingratiative purpose and their behaviour is not so unlike his own experience that he cannot understand and even condone it now. Their world is crumbling; so far as they can tell their only prospect is one of annihilation; their disobedience, cutting them off from God, leaves them only each other to turn to. Is it so very unnatural of them to seize upon an objective feature of their happiness, upon each other (1037), with a new kind of urgency and desperation? To point to the unpleasant jocosity with which they do so (1024-6) is not to dispose of this interpretation. That, like their lust itself, is easily ascribed to the intoxicating operation of the fruit (1008) and need not distort one's appreciation of their true condition. They are lonely, apprehensive, bewildered, and the comparison Milton makes between Adam and Samson (1059-63) serves only to emphasize the complexity of their case. Eve is not a 'Harlot', as Delilah is said to be, nor is the passion between Adam and herself properly comparable with Samson's desire and Delilah's scornful provocativeness. As Milton himself said earlier in the poem (iv. 767) the sexual unions of a harlot are

K

merely 'Casual'. It is the last word one would apply to Adam and Eve's embraces here.

What about their quarrelling then, with which Book Nine concludes? Though the reader's reaction to it is not perhaps quite Milton's it does not seem to be much less reproachful. Milton evidently sees their quarrel as an external sign of their inner turmoil, the 'high Passions, Anger, Hate, Mistrust, Suspicion, Discord' (1123-4) which begin now to reduce their minds to a level of confusion much like Satan's. For him their recriminations reflect their abandonment of Right Reason, and thus their fall from Grace. The reader, though he sees this too, is more concerned about the dislike that seems to have sprung up between them. Their prelapsarian relationship of trust and understanding appears to have been shattered, and the remarks that they address to each other are calculated to wound, and wound unfairly. Adam reproves Eve for 'that strange Desire of wandring this unhappie Morn' (1135-6), misrepresenting her original intention so as to magnify her responsibility; and Eve, stung by this 'touch of blame', forgetting how she persuaded him to subdue his misgivings, ungenerously retorts that he should never have let her go (1155-61). Justifiably 'then first incenst' Adam rounds on her in turn, demanding whether this is her gratitude for the devotion he has shown, to blame him for the fact that she has fallen (1162-70). Some glimmering of reason appears fleetingly in his speech when he admits that 'perhaps I also err'd' (1177-8), but this is immediately extinguished in his denunciation of women in general (1182-6), a denunciation which is all the more irrational in view of his limited experience with them. Irrationality, however, is the least of a reader's worries. What really disturbs him is the impression that their love, so recently proclaimed and vindicated, has been utterly undermined. I do not think it is possible to shrug off this impression, or to pretend that Adam and Eve's dissension is other than a shock—our first real intimation, perhaps, of the banefulness of their Fall. One may indicate the comparative restraint with which, even in anger, they choose their words; one may point out that it is a common enough experience to quarrel, and that, in the words if not the sense of Shakespeare's Ulysses, 'One touch of nature makes the whole world kin'; one may cite the shrewd opinion of Terence that lovers renew their love by quarrelling: *amantium irae amoris integratiost.* The fact remains that Adam and Eve are here in conflict with those very values which they themselves have symbolized, the values of gentleness, loyalty, and love. Whatever excuses the reader can find for their wantonness, and for whatever good reasons, it must distress and estrange him to watch them behaving like this.

How far the estrangement goes is another question. If we ask ourselves whether the whole force of Book Nine and its predecessors is finally altered and weakened, whether we are persuaded to shift our allegiance from the appealing creatures of Earth to the austere and sometimes suspicious inhabitants of Heaven, the questions soon answer themselves. If it were simply a matter of Heaven and Earth being balanced against each other like the ends of a see-saw then no doubt the debasement of Adam and Eve, however temporary, would result in a corresponding elevation in our opinion of God. But the position is much more complex now, obliging our thoughts to go ranging back through the epic in search of the true culprit for what has happened. Adam and Eve's disharmony is plainly a consequence of their Fall, but of what exactly their Fall is a consequence is far from clear. Since the list of possible culprits is none too short—the pair themselves, and therefore Satan, and therefore Sin, Gabriel, and even Michael—it is easy to feel bewildered, and one can imagine the comment of an inattentive reader: 'God alone knows why they've fallen.' Perhaps the best way to shock him into attending would be to point out that an alert and perceptive reader's response might be summarized in the selfsame words.

Chapter Seven

CONSEQUENCES OF THE FALL

EVERYTHING changes after the Fall: even the verse loses much of the lustre it has lately recovered. Yet by this stage the most important change of all may be unattainable. The reader's attitude to God and to Man has had sufficient time, and sufficient cause, to settle along an axis of distaste and affection, and three more books are a narrow margin in which to unsettle and reform it. For a critic the main interest of these books lies less in their incidents or their poetry—both sometimes a little tedious— than in determining the extent of such a reform. His judgements, if they are to carry any weight, must apply to the epic as a whole and not just to certain sections, no matter how large. Before coming to this central problem, however, it seems advisable to give some account, as brief as may be, of the harvest which accrues to Satan and his followers as a result of their success. One can contrive a rough subdivision of the consequences of the Fall according to where they operate: in Hell, in Heaven, and of course on Earth.

I

As it affects the denizens of Hell the Fall has two chief consequences, one minor and one major. The minor consequence is that it provides the occasion for Sin and Death's reappearance, and thus for the return of the allegorical element which, as was noted earlier, is so unsatisfactory in Book Two. Allegory proper, it is fair to say, is used rather sparingly in *Paradise Lost*, being mostly confined to the sections involving Sin and Death. But a tendency

in the direction of allegory—towards personification and the
embodiment of abstractions—is so marked throughout the poem
that it has come to be thought of as an essential part of the heroic
style, a view which Homer's verse, for instance, would hardly
support. The bent betrays itself in occasional imprecisions of
phrase, like 'the sole [for 'soles'] Of unblest feet' (i. 237-8), or
'servitude' for 'servants' (xii. 132), where realized abstractions
replace realities, but it shows up more clearly in Milton's persistent
hypostatizations: when 'grace' becomes a 'winged messenger',
like Raphael (iii. 229), for example, or when 'Miserie' becomes
Death's herald (ix. 12-13), or Adam and Eve's prayers take form as
some kind of 'Dimentionless' birds (xi. 14-20). Though not always
objectionable, there are two objections that can be made to it.
First, it often results in clumsiness, as when Chaos, previously as
much a king as a place, is credited with a 'rebounding surge'
(x. 417), or the personification Shame is made the basis for an
awkward play on words (ix. 1058-9). Secondly, it encourages a
strain in the poetry which is turgid and tortuous, which lacks the
vividness and energy it should have. Consider the description of
the stranding of Noah's ark in Book Eleven:

> . . . The cleer Sun on his wide watrie Glass
> Gaz'd hot, and of the fresh Wave largely drew,
> As after thirst, which made thir flowing shrink
> From standing lake to tripping ebbe, that stole
> With soft foot towards the deep, who now had stopt
> His Sluces, as the Heav'n his windows shut.
> The Ark no more now flotes, but seems on ground
> Fast on the top of som high mountain fixt.
> And now the tops of Hills as Rocks appeer;
> With clamor thence the rapid Currents drive
> Towards the retreating Sea thir furious tyde.   (844-54)

Observe how at first the verse is clotted with semi-personifica-
tions: the sun staring into a mirror and then sucking up the waters,
the ebb 'tripping . . . With soft foot', the deep like a farmer
engaged in some mysterious form of irrigation, and Heaven a

householder shutting out the rain.[1] Only when the verse shakes off
this integument of half-formed and jumbled images does the
scene come into focus, and only then does it come to life: the
rising crests of the hills, the run-off of water plunging and frothing
down the valleys, and the line of the subsiding sea.

Granted a tendency in the poem to modulate into this idiom,
and to present symbolic incidents like the appearance of God's
golden scales in the sky (iv. 997), it is scarcely surprising that
allegorical figures should also be introduced. If they were judiciously handled this would not matter, but the trouble with Sin and
Death is that they are not. The chief problem raised by their first
appearance, without a doubt, is that of Satan's escape from Hell.
On the one hand, if Hell's gates are really meant to 'prohibit all
egress', as Satan says they are (ii. 437), then his escape represents a
victory over God, and his sneer later on is fully justified: 'let him
surer barr His Iron Gates, if he intends our stay In that dark
durance' (iv. 897-9). On the other hand, if God is merely giving
Satan the rope to hang himself, and to hoist the Son's colours aloft,
then he appears to be doing it with a notable lack of frankness
(ii. 774-6; iii. 80-4), and with so slight a regard for Man that he is
content to offer him no more than a slim chance of salvation in
exchange for losing Paradise. Either way, Satan's opponent seems
much less magnificent than he should. With Sin and Death's
reappearance this problem returns to haunt the fringes of a reader's
mind, and other problems soon arrive to join it. One is the
artistic problem of anticlimax. Though some degree of interest
attaches to allegorical actions like the building of the bridge from

---

[1] No one could call this Homeric: it is Silver Latin at best. Compare Lucan,
De Bello Civili, ix. 313-14:

> sed rapidus Titan ponto sua lumina pascens
> aequora subduxit zonae vicina perustae,

a passage the context of which recalls Milton's 'Boggie *Syrtis*' at ii. 939; or this
from the same poem:

> flammiger an Titan, ut alentes hauriat undas,
> erigat Oceanum fluctusque ad sidera ducat.   (i. 415-16)

Heaven's windows however, as Professor Hughes has observed, are biblical (Gen.
8:2).

the 'fenceless World' to Hell (x. 282 ff.), and even to allegorical statements like 'For Death from Sin no power can separate' (251), it is faint beside the engrossed attention given to Adam and Eve's misfortunes in Book Nine. Another is the more troublesome problem—equally troublesome in Book Two—of maintaining the allegory at the proper level of coherence, without falling into discrepancies or contradictions. It is a serious matter and, to judge from Milton's handling of it, far from easy to control. Certain apparent inconsistencies in the presentation of Sin and Death at this point are admittedly deliberate, being meant to show the exhilaration and amity kindled in the creatures of Hell by Satan's success. When Death forgets to torment Sin and becomes her docile assistant (265-71) it is because he has scented 'with delight' the smell of carnage, and when Sin is described as Satan's 'faire Inchanting Daughter' (352-3) it is because Satan now sees her like that, made handsome by his joy. But other inconsistencies are not so easy to defend, and some are simply clumsy. One example, which shows how hard it is to blend two distinct levels of discourse in a single narrative like Milton's, concerns the 'wings' which Adam and Eve feel 'breeding' in them after their Fall (ix. 1010) and which Sin and Death in turn feel 'growing' within them at about the same time (x. 244). The former are acceptably metaphorical, but to our surprise the latter are found to be physical appendages, permitting Sin and Death to fly (284). This new ability to take wing is itself not very happily conceived, inviting the reader to wonder whether Sin's hell-hounds accompany her in flight; and the other ability now conferred on them, to penetrate Satan's disguises (330-1), is equally unsatisfactory, Milton having earlier laid down that such clairvoyance was the prerogative of God alone (iii. 684). Even less convincing is the metamorphosis which Death seems to have undergone since Book Two. Once a shapeless shadow (ii. 666-70) he now has at least one 'Nostril' (x. 280) and will in due course, as in the Apocalypse, bestride a horse (589-90). Once uncontrollably voracious (ii. 845-8) his appetite seems to have lost much of its edge (xi. 491-3). And once apparently Sin's only child, apart from the hell-hounds, he now has a sister, Discord (x. 707-8), but a sister who was earlier a member of the court of Chaos and no more a relative of his than Chance or Demogorgon (ii. 967). Such inconsistencies, it may be said, are all but inevitable when resort is had to allegory. The plea is a very dubious one, but even if it is admitted that merely affords a further reason why Milton might well have dispensed with the allegory here.

The major consequence which the Fall has for the creatures of Hell concerns the punishment meted out to them, and it is even more disturbing. Any normally attentive reader remembers from Book Two the predictions made by Beelzebub, Satan, and Sin regarding the advantages that will accrue to Hell if Man can be made to fall (397-400, 840-4, 866-70), and he is also likely to remember God's declaration, after the War in Heaven, that Man is to be created so that his progeny can eventually replace the angels whom Satan has seduced (vii. 150-61). Now he finds Sin claiming that the predicted advantages are within reach, and that God's plan has been upset:

> Thou hast atchiev'd our libertie, confin'd
> Within Hell Gates till now, thou us impow'rd
> To fortifie thus farr, and overlay
> With this portentous Bridge the dark Abyss.
> Thine now is all this World, thy vertue hath won
> What thy hands builded not, thy Wisdom gain'd
> With odds what Warr hath lost, and fully aveng'd
> Our foile in Heav'n; here thou shalt Monarch reign,
> There didst not; there let him still Victor sway,
> As Battel hath adjudg'd, from this new World
> Retiring, by his own doom alienated.　　　　(x. 368-78)

On the face of it, the claim is indefeasible: Satan *has* achieved these results, just as he hoped to do. Well may he reassure his army that their titles, once in doubt (ii. 310-13; v. 772-4), are once more valid and incontestable (x. 460-2). Well may he triumph (500), demanding of them, 'A World who would not purchase with a bruise?' Appreciating the extent of his success, the reader looks for some convincing indication that it is actually a hollow one, that all this jubilation is out of place. Yet the fact of the matter is that the real punishment in store for the devils lies beyond the scope of the poem: it can only be prophetically hinted, not dramatized or demonstrated, and for that reason it seems remote and disproportionately mild. God, soon to be seen destroying all mankind save Noah's family for their depravity, seems for the present almost indifferent to Satan's. Milton obviously realized that Satan was likely to seem all too successful here, for one can see him using all his resources to convert the reader's reaction into one of derision. He gives Satan the child's ambition, invisibility (448), decries his glory as 'false glitter' (452), and makes him pad out his account of his exploits with boastful lies (478-9). None of these devices being anywhere near adequate he has, of necessity, to go farther, and accordingly he devotes over seventy lines (504-77) to describing the discomfiture which now descends on the host of Hell. They turn into snakes; they hiss each other; and they eat 'bitter Ashes'. One can concede that much of this is finely done —the grotesque account of Satan's transformation at 511-15 is particularly courageous, and wholly effective—but one has also to protest that it is not enough, not nearly enough. Satan's crime must be one of the gravest ever committed; yet to present his punishment dramatically the poet can offer no more than a charade. When the devils are transformed into serpents it is as if a political cartoonist were caricaturing his party's only too successful opponents after an election.[1] When a grove of trees suddenly springs up 'with this thir change' (548) God becomes a conjurer, manipulating one of those collapsible, suddenly blooming bouquets. When they chew the fruit of the trees and find it ashes he becomes a schoolboy deluding his rivals with soap-filled chocolates. And when they are actually allowed to resume 'thir lost shape, permitted' (574) the whole episode collapses into farcical triviality. A world who would not purchase with a jape? The section concludes with a mention of a false mythological version of the devils' punishment (578-84) but in comparison with the

---

[1] Cf. Waldock, *Paradise Lost and Its Critics*, pp. 91-2.

'authentic' version that has been given it is positively credible, and certainly much less incompatible with God's dignity. The retrospective effect is to weaken all Milton's qualifications regarding the myths he mentions—'Erring' (i. 747), 'If true, here only' (iv. 251), 'though but feignd' (iv. 706), and the rest—and to drag the Christian story down to the same level of feigning and error.

II

Few readers will agree with Satan that God's estrangement from Man over the Fall is laughable (x. 488) but it is distinctly suspicious. By this stage God's conduct has come to seem quite unworthy of him, and it is to be expected that the reader should find himself keeping a wary eye on it, almost as a ratepayer might watch an arrogantly self-righteous mayor loitering in an unlit street. Is there much in what he sees of God during the rest of the poem to reassure him? I want for the present, so far as is possible, to confine myself to the individual impressions made by God and by Man during the final stages of the epic, so that my first concern will be with God's actual appearances, with the glimpses that we catch of Heaven in Books Ten and Eleven. They are important, for only in them are his reactions directly presented, rather than indirectly explained. Finally, having assessed the behaviour both of God and of Man, we can come to the central question of the relationship that now exists between the two.

Intolerantly speaking, with the intolerance induced by the poem itself, God's first reaction to the Fall, in Book Ten, might almost be one of pleasure. He can thunder with good reason now (x. 31-3), and he can apply his whole attention to the congenial matter of judgement (48 ff.). The impression is unfair, but it is partly borne out by his readiness to distort the facts of the Fall—as if, enjoying his anger, he did not wish to moderate it, even for the sake of truth. He makes no reference at all to Eve's wish to improve the quality of her companionship, or to Adam's devotion, and can find nothing more in their actions than an affront to himself: Man has been 'seduc't And flatter'd out of all, believing lies Against his Maker' (41-3). So brief are the glimpses of God provided in Book Ten that there is scarcely time to notice much more than this, unless it is the suggestion of uneasiness with which he justifies his foretelling of the Fall and lack of responsibility for it (40-7) or the intemperacy of his speech (629-33). When in Book Eleven he reappears, however, our view of him is rather more sustained. What sort of impression does he make?

Again perhaps one senses his inability to report his facts with perfect accuracy (xi. 61), or to maintain the 'serene' level on which his speech begins (48-57), but what is far more striking is the almost obsessive craving he displays to justify his own part in the Fall. Determined that his angels shall not misunderstand him he summons them all from their 'fellowships of joy' into his presence, points out to them just where he stands, and then apparently sends them about their business once again. The episode seems doubly inept. In the first place God is going to inordinate trouble to defend himself, so that one is tempted to imagine the angels' soldierly comments; in the second, the defence he offers is far from conclusive, so that the whole manoeuvre appears to be a waste of time. His suggestion that Adam and Eve must be removed from Eden lest they now

> Reach also of the Tree of Life, and eat,
> And live for ever, dream at least to live
> For ever   (94-6)

is too indecisive to be convincing, particularly since he has himself just advanced a more satisfactory reason for their banishment (48-57), and his claim that their contrition is due to his 'motions' in them rather than their own volition (90-1) seems downright unfair. Despite Milton's evasive references to 'Grace' (3, 23) the reader remains convinced that in Book Ten he has seen the humans repenting, not being made to repent, and indeed this conviction is fully supported by the poet's own doctrine of Free Will. Why should Adam's bad deeds be attributed to his personal and un-fettered choice while his good ones are attributed to God? We wonder why, if God is now conferring a special degree of 'Strength' upon the humans (138), he was so chary of doing it while they were being tempted. Why also should Michael be instructed to inform them of God's covenant only 'If patiently thy bidding they obey' (112)? Granted God's claim that they are now behaving according to his motions, and likely to be 'variable and vain' without them (90-3), this condition regarding their patience can be fulfilled only if he himself gives them the patience to fulfil it. For God to present himself as a landowner jealous of his orchards' fruits, as he does at 123-5, is unimpressive enough; that he should seem a casuist is intolerable.

The most suitable term for all this is surely Milton's own: shameful garrulity.[1] God's speech raises more problems than it solves and the reader is left wondering why it was not omitted, as other speeches with better claims to inclusion were without loss at i. 529-30 and x. 865. But there are further reasons for finding Milton's presentation of the Deity in these books unsatisfactory, and the occasion for one of them follows hard upon God's speech to the angels, soon after attention has been switched to Eve:

> Nigh in her sight
> The Bird of *Jove*, stoopt from his aerie tour,
> Two Birds of gayest plume before him drove:
> Down from a Hill the Beast that reigns in Woods,
> First Hunter then, pursu'd a gentle brace,
> Goodliest of all the Forrest, Hart and Hinde.   (xi. 184-9)

On one level this is straightforward fact, one earthly consequence of the Fall being to destroy the harmony prevailing among the animals. On another, however, the eagle and lion are obviously meant to symbolize God, and it is noteworthy that Milton should represent his justice so harshly, as something predatory and cruel. The symbolism is so apt as to be arresting. God shows traces of indecision or volatility (xi. 885) and even of feeble credulity (xii. 51-2) after the Fall, but the chief impression he makes is of grimness and rigour, an almost complete unwillingness to consider

---

[1] *Samson Agonistes*, 491.

the claims which Adam and Eve might have on his lenity. Nor is the reason for this impression far to seek. As in Book Three the answer lies in Milton's presentation of the Son, the incipiently human figure who, far from manifesting all his Father's virtues (x. 66), has simply deprived him of them. The Son's existence in the poem is exemplary, but it is also parasitic: those qualities which might have redeemed the portraiture of God are stripped away and vested almost exclusively in him. The irony is that God himself should contribute to this arrangement, as he does in lines like these:

> Easie it might be seen that I intend
> Mercie collegue with Justice, sending thee
> Mans Friend, his Mediator, his design'd
> Both Ransom and Redeemer voluntarie,
> And destin'd Man himself to judge Man fall'n. (x. 58-62)

Surely the implication is that if God were himself to judge the humans their punishment might be very much more severe? What follows does much to strengthen such a view. Unlike his Father the Son is 'milde' (67, 96) and quite devoid of 'wrauth' (95); he has to 'appease' God (79); and he tactfully persuades him to permit the judgement to be delivered in private, so that Adam and Eve may be spared unnecessary humiliation (80-2). During the judgement itself, which comes next, all talk of wrath or thunder is suppressed, Milton's presentation of the Son being consistently a matter of bare speech, with suggestions of gentleness (105, 118) and a timely reference to the human Jesus (182-91) to indicate just what tone he is using. And the same is true of the treatment of the Son after his sentence has been pronounced, where again one can see his pity (211), the humility which, when incarnate, he will retain (211-19), and the philanthropy that causes him to shield the humans, like an ally, 'from his Fathers sight' (223). Later, when Adam and Eve are standing 'in lowliest plight repentant' (xi. 1), a condition to soften the hardest of hearts, we are shocked to find that the Son must 'intercede' before his Father can bring himself to hear their prayers (21, 30-6), particularly since these have been

extravagantly commended (9-20). The effect is very different from
the idea so movingly expressed in the First Epistle of St. John:

> And if any man sin, we have an advocate with the Father, Jesus
> Christ the righteous: And he is the propitiation for our sins.   (2: 1-2)

Here it is more as though a tactful Cordelia were trying to wring
some concession of decency from a reluctant and oafish Lear.
Very occasionally Milton seems to make some kind of effort to
palliate the impression left by God, as he does at xi. 181, where
God's inflexibility is neutrally attributed to 'Fate'. For the most
part, however, he is content to degrade him. The pure wine of
divine virtue being decanted into the vessel provided by the Son
only the lees are left God's vault to brag of. And a bitter brew
they prove.

III

Meanwhile on Earth a golden world is rapidly becoming
brazen. It is not necessary to detail all the changes which now take
place in the terrestrial universe: some of the most striking are
effectively summarized, though with one cosmographical solecism
(680-5), at x. 651-714. More significant are the changes which are
taking place in Adam and Eve themselves, it being with them
rather than Eden that a reader's interest really lies. Admittedly
the macrocosmic changes in some degree reflect the microcosmic
(cf. 714-17). If Eden's nights have lost their wholesomeness and
now bring 'damps and dreadful gloom' that is partly because
Adam's conscience is troubled, a prey to nocturnal fears (846-50),
and if 'fierce antipathie' (709) now divides the animals in the
Garden something rather similar divides the hearts of Adam and
Eve: their 'plaint', for example, is significantly 'various', each
bemoaning his or her fate without much thought for the other
(343). But this is a roundabout way of presenting their changed
condition, and the reader is naturally more intent on their actual
appearances. Only by watching them closely can he determine
their state with anything like precision, and only by determining
it with some precision can he clarify his attitude towards their Fall.

A more direct method which Milton uses to show that Adam and Eve have been corrupted is the obvious one: he tells us that they have been. When the Son summons them into his presence to judge them they are described like this:

> Love was not in thir looks, either to God
> Or to each other, but apparent guilt,
> And shame, and perturbation, and despaire,
> Anger, and obstinacie, and hate, and guile. (x. 111-14)

So far so good, or bad. Yet in fact, whether because their attitude immediately undergoes some adjustment, or because Milton himself cannot rest the matter there, we see surprisingly little of passions like 'Anger' and 'hate' in them, and indeed it is impossible to overlook the contrition, unselfishness, and humility with which they are credited during the whole course of Book Ten. Eve is 'abasht' at having to confess her fault (161); she wants to take the whole burden of guilt upon herself (932-6); she reveals how pathetically dependent she is on Adam (914-27); and she assumes without question that she has forfeited his love, so that it will be necessary for her to win it back again (972-3). For his part Adam is so ashamed of himself that even after the Son's judgement his remorse continues to torment him (723-7); he is aghast to realize that Eve's and his punishment is entailed, and will descend to their posterity (725-41, 818-22); and he too is ready, in an endearingly gentle speech, to take sole responsibility for their sin (947-57). These are substantial acts and utterances, not mere imputations, and they do not chime with Milton's earlier reports that Adam and Eve are angry and guileful, or 'manifold in sin' (16). Even when Adam reproves Eve for her frailty or foolishness the reproofs are so overstated (868-9, 873-88, 1041-6) that instead of agreeing with them the reader is encouraged to take her part. Such accusations, though we are prepared for them, are in any case rare outside the quarrel in Book Nine and a single speech of Adam's in Book Ten (867-908). Much commoner are self-accusations, in which the humans refuse to extenuate their own guilt. Eve makes a half-hearted attempt to excuse herself at x. 916, when she says that she fell 'unweeting', but for the rest she shows an exemplary readiness to admit her fault, and even perhaps to exaggerate it (x. 969, xi. 163-9). Adam, though his transgression was much more dubious than hers, is utterly humble and penitent (xi. 331-3, 526), and when he condemns himself for having sought 'Forbidd'n knowledge by forbidd'n means' (xii. 278-9), foolishly aspiring beyond his proper limitations (xii. 560), the reproaches strike us as largely unrelated to his disobedience and quite unnecessarily severe.

The point is that the Fall has only a very temporary effect on Adam and Eve's personal qualities, and that Milton takes care during the last three books to show that it has, to show that they are still just as modest and as decent as they were during Books Four and Five. There is conclusive proof of this in one passage, for it shows him deliberately modifying the biblical account in order to put Adam in a more favourable light. This is when the Son asks whether Adam has eaten the forbidden fruit. In the Book of Genesis his reply is churlish and cowardly: 'The woman whom thou gavest to be with me, she gave me of the tree, and I did eat' (3: 12). In *Paradise Lost* the equivalent response has been carefully expanded (x. 125-43), and the poet's concern to minimize any prejudice or hostility to which it might give rise can be clearly seen. The question thus poses itself why he should want to present the transgressors so sympathetically, why in fact he should systematically undermine his own assertion that they have yielded to 'Anger, and obstinacie, and hate, and guile'.

Two answers come to mind almost at once, one doctrinal and one artistic. In the first place, if Adam and Eve's Fall corrupted them too thoroughly then the Atonement would be unmerited and God's mercy might well seem indiscriminate and careless rather than just. In the second, if they were to continue at the unprepossessing level they reached at the end of Book Nine the reader's interest in them, and therefore in the concluding books of the poem, would very soon evaporate. One does not want to underestimate these motives, which are straightforward, but the thoroughness with which Milton lavishes his charity on the human

couple, both during the Fall itself and now again during its after-
math, suggests that another motive is also present, one which is
more positive and yet more difficult to describe. A preliminary
fact that seems to be deducible from the exordium to Book Seven
(24-8) is that some considerable time had elapsed between the
writing of the first lines of the poem, with their undertaking to
'justifie the wayes of God to men', and the writing of the last books.
The suggestion of other passages is that during the interval Milton's
proposed theme underwent no little modification, and that the
magnetism attracting him to his human protagonists so displaced
his stance that it became a matter almost of justifying the ways of
men to God. In speaking of the tractability of his human material
I have already instanced the lines at the beginning of Book Nine
in which, God's ways forgotten, he speaks of human patience and
fortitude as especially suitable subjects for 'Heroic Song' (25-33).
What is likely to strike a reader going through the last three books
is that their central subject seems to be precisely that: the 'Patience
and Heroic Martyrdom' displayed by Adam and Eve in the face
of the tragedy which, as was predicted at ix. 6, has overtaken them.
What else is Adam invoking (apart from our sympathies, with his
'blam'd enough elsewhere') when he addresses Eve like this?

> But rise, let us no more contend, nor blame
> Each other, blam'd enough elsewhere, but strive
> In offices of Love, how we may light'n
> Each others burden in our share of woe.   (x. 958-61)

What else is Michael recommending when he tells Adam that
he must learn 'True patience'?—

> True patience, and to temper joy with fear
> And pious sorrow, equally enur'd
> By moderation either state to beare,
> Prosperous or adverse.   (xi. 361-4)

What else, if not this, is the discussion of the 'paradise within'
(xii. 587) all about? It is as though the seed of *Paradise Regain'd*
were already germinating in the poet's mind, even before the

L

anticipation of its action at xi. 381-4. A counter-subject has appeared in the poem's music, and it is so rich and insistent that it drowns the subject originally proposed.

IV

This deduction is worth pondering for the light it throws on the incidents and speeches reported at the conclusion of *Paradise Lost*. Let me repeat that I am not concerned to ascribe intentions to the poet, whether conscious or unconscious. To speak of a change in his subject is not to lose sight of the fact that it might be almost completely inadvertent, a consequence simply of the artistic material that he was handling: *der Stoff dichtet*, as one might say. Whether Milton actually lost interest in the ways of God is a question which can only lead to irresponsible speculation. Whether his epic shows signs of doing so is a valid critical inquiry, verifiable from the text. My contention is that, like 'Lycidas',[1] the end of *Paradise Lost* appears to have both a nominal and a *de facto* subject, and that the reader is naturally more conscious of the one than of the other. But this must be proposed less cursorily. Let us look at those sections, finally, where God and Man are seen in some kind of direct relationship, for it is in them that the change in emphasis can be most tangibly felt. Since we are concerned with a single poem I continue to assume that the reader will be influenced by what he has seen and heard of God in the preceding three quarters of it, and that his reactions to these sections will be coloured accordingly.

The first passage of real importance here is Adam's 'sad complaint' in Book Ten, especially that portion of it which is frankly preoccupied with God's treatment of him:

> Did I request thee, Maker, from my Clay
> To mould me Man, did I sollicite thee
> From darkness to promote me, or here place
> In this delicious Garden? as my Will

---

[1] The standard account of 'Lycidas' is in E. M. W. Tillyard's *Milton* (London, 1946), pp. 79-85.

> Concurd not to my being, it were but right
> And equal to reduce me to my dust,
> Desirous to resigne, and render back
> All I receav'd, unable to performe
> Thy terms too hard, by which I was to hold
> The good I sought not. To the loss of that,
> Sufficient penaltie, why hast thou added
> The sense of endless woes? inexplicable
> Thy Justice seems.   (743-55)

One does not need to maintain that this is a complete answer to
the Christian doctrines of Free Will and Original Sin to claim that,
in its context, it is dangerously plausible. So skilfully has Milton
presented Eve's temptation, so wholeheartedly has he allowed us
to endorse Adam's decision to fall with her, that the protest
against a God whose terms are 'too hard', beyond the humans'
capacity, finds a ready echo in the reader's mind. So appealingly
contrite are the delinquents allowed to appear that God's decision
to inflict 'endless woes' on their descendants, too, is bound to seem
'inexplicable', if not downright vindictive, like punishing the
serpent for Satan's misdeeds. Far from justifying them, the passage
subjects the ways of God to an uncomfortably candid scrutiny.
Adam goes on to counter his own arguments in a way that
Milton presumably intended to be final, but after such an out-
burst the refutation sounds far too docile, and confused besides:

> Yet to say truth, too late,
> I thus contest; then should have been refusd
> Those terms whatever, when they were propos'd:
> Thou didst accept them; wilt thou enjoy the good,
> Then cavil the conditions? and though God
> Made thee without thy leave, what if thy Son
> Prove disobedient, and reprov'd, retort
> Wherefore didst thou beget me? I sought it not:
> Wouldst thou admit for his contempt of thee
> That proud excuse?   (755-64)

Surely this is sophistical, and sophistical at all points. First, to
speak of God's having 'propos'd' the terms of human existence,

as if he had made a tender of them, is incorrect and misleading. Had Adam in fact 'refusd' his existence before this stage his behaviour would have been both unnatural and absurd. Secondly, considering the span of life he has so far enjoyed—at best a matter of weeks—to speak of his happiness as if it somehow balanced the unhappiness that is now to descend upon himself and his posterity (758-9) is disproportionate, to say the least. Finally, the analogy with a disobedient son is imprecise to the point of being false. God created Adam in a form where, as he says, and as events have proved, his 'Will Concurd not to [his] being', and created him 'of choice' in such a form (766). A son's disobedience may be attributable in part to the acts of his father, for example to his harshness or inconsistency, but no father *creates* a disobedient son in any sense analogous to this. The upshot is only to strengthen a reader's trust in the complaints which Adam is trying to refute. When he concludes this part of his speech with the decision 'I submit, his doom is fair' (769) one can applaud his submissiveness but it is surely very difficult to share his point of view.

A factor that undoubtedly contributes to this heterodox interpretation is Adam's solicitude for his descendants, the fulcrum of benevolence on which his whole soliloquy turns. One tends to forget, in reading, just how easy it would have been for the poem to leave its human readers cursing Adam and Eve for their legacy of death and disorder, but to bear the point in mind is to appreciate how well they are shielded from our disapproval, and in particular how much better they are shielded than God himself. For one thing, there is Adam's courageous refusal to extenuate his fault, at times a refusal which, if anything, can only strike us as too courageous, too severe:

> On mee, mee onely, as the sourse and spring
> Of all corruption, all the blame lights due.   (832-3)

For another, there is the human couple's passionate concern for their progeny's welfare—'miserable it is To be to others cause of misery'—a concern which is clear enough in Adam's soliloquy but

even clearer when Eve makes her proposal either to remain child-
less or to kill themselves (967-1006). For yet another, there is
Adam's touchingly loyal attempt to prove that God's judgement
on them is 'mild' (1048-59), an endeavour that obliges him to
omit all reference to their mortality, to the suspended sentence of
death which has been passed on them. No such virtues can be
detected in God. On the contrary he is almost recklessly inculpated
when Eve is allowed to call Satan 'a Foe by doom express assign'd
us' (926), and many small but significant touches suggest that he
has become Man's enemy, one whom it is almost necessary for the
humans to plot against, and that Heaven is a hostile camp between
which and Earth such an arrangement as a 'Truce' is now quite
natural (x. 959, 1022-4; xi. 244, 311-13). It is true that this stark
contrast is mitigated during Book Eleven, when the polarizing
agency supplied by the man-angel Michael sets up more complex
undercurrents in the presentation of Adam and Eve. Here the
behaviour of the humans is sometimes undignified, as in Eve's
almost comic 'audible lament' offstage (266), or rather tedious, as
in Adam's tearful reactions to futurity (495-9, 674, 754-8), while
their speech is sometimes, in Eve's case, foolishly hyperbolic (268)
and, in Adam's, so smug as to suggest hypocrisy (632-3). Though
they are disconcerting such lapses are not, however, enough to
disturb for more than a moment the general impression we have
formed of God and Man, particularly since other passages in Book
Eleven are close enough to the implications of Book Ten to seem
like confirmations of them. Michael's suggestion that Adam has
'conspir'd' with the snake, for example (426), is quite unwarranted
and therefore repels us, while Adam's 'plaint renew'd' again raises
the thorny question as to just how fully the humans may be said to
have accepted the 'propos'd' terms of their creation:

> Why is life giv'n
> To be thus wrested from us? rather why
> Obtruded on us thus? who if we knew
> What we receive, would either not accept
> Life offer'd, or soon beg to lay it down,
> Glad to be so dismist in peace.   (502-7)

Here too the impulsive reactions of Adam at times seem natural and generous compared with the cool circumspection of the angel (593-606), and when he does behave ungenerously it is on Eve's account, not Heaven's, that the reader feels indignant with him (632-3). In view of all that has been said concerning the mortality of Adam's posterity it is possible, too, to feel that Enoch's exemption from death (709) is rather suspicious, and that once again God has not been perfectly frank in setting out the full conditions of his will.

Book Twelve, some will say, effectively dispels all the reservations about God which its predecessors have encouraged. Certainly it would be a grossly insensitive reader who could ignore the art with which Michael's account of the Atonement, the *felix culpa*, is gradually insinuated into his historical narrative, like a symphonic theme almost imperceptibly disengaging itself from the cloudy sonorities in which it has been shrouded, gathering power with every reappearance, and finally blazing out in the full splendour of a major and unequivocal assertion. Certainly too it is impossible to disregard the weight of the assertion: the poignancy of the crucified Redeemer's death, the inexhaustible mercy which his sacrifice releases, the charity of God.

> For this he shall live hated, be blasphem'd,
> Seis'd on by force, judg'd, and to death condemnd
> A shameful and accurst, naild to the Cross
> By his own Nation, slaine for bringing Life;
> But to the Cross he nailes thy Enemies,
> The Law that is against thee, and the sins
> Of all mankinde, with him there crucifi'd,
> Never to hurt them more who rightly trust
> In this his satisfaction.   (411-19)

The difficulty, nevertheless, is that a reader is expected not only to acclaim the Son for his Redemption, which we unhesitatingly do, but to feel overwhelming gratitude to God for permitting it, which we do not. I am not saying that the Atonement is extraneous to Milton's subject. On the contrary it has been referred to again and again during the course of the poem: i. 4-5, i. 217-19,

ii. 385-6, iii. 274 ff., &c. Nor am I denying the artistic irony with which Satan's original plan has been reversed. But the reader's orientation towards God must also be reversed if the climax here is to achieve its full effect, and that is surely asking too much of him. Michael's discussion of Law has harped on the idea that God will prepare Man to accept his Son's triumph, that nothing is to be left to chance (xii. 285-306), and inevitably we have found ourselves remembering God's behaviour during and after the War, the circumspection with which the whole history of men and angels seemed to be 'governd' towards a single end: the glorification of his Son. Inevitably, too, we recall God's restless self-defences in Book Three and Book Eleven. How, with all this and more against him, can we now accept him as Milton requires, with unalloyed gratitude and worship? The most we can do is to credit the Atonement as if exclusively to the Son, thus despoiling God of yet another of his excellences, perhaps the most creditable of all.

It would be absurd to suppose that Milton divined this result. He took for his subject a myth, not a history, an inference by which men sought to explain the seething complexity of their own natures, and like a mathematician proving a converse he had then to reverse the process of inference, accepting the myth as history and projecting it forward so as to link it up again with the facts from which it had been inferred. It was a projection of almost impossible delicacy, where the smallest blurs and uncertainties in the original inference, or in his comprehension of it, were bound to be magnified and distorted. Yet it is hard to believe that he fully appreciated its delicacy, or that he understood just how serious the distortion often was. What he did realize, perhaps, was that Michael's prophecy of the Redemption did not provide the ultimate climax which it was meant to provide, that the emotional force it released, though powerful, was neither so free nor so full as it should have been. Even at a moment of incandescence like this there had to be hesitations and pauses, where the doctrine could be more precisely defined (410, 427). With a true poet's instinct therefore, an instinct that seldom if ever deserted him when the

ending of a poem was in question, he turned back to the real
emotional centre which his subject had acquired, writing that
magnificent conclusion which, even after yearly repetitions, any
teacher may be forgiven for mistrusting his voice to carry quite
steadily. Only in a last glimpse of Adam and Eve going hand in
hand could the whole sweep and utterance of the poem be clinched.
Only in a human picture could the sadness and the majesty of its
story be caught and held.

Chapter Eight

EPILOGUE

CRITICISM's standard is that of a reasonable man: the axiom is worth repeating. There will always be unreasonable men to make unreasonable claims for *Paradise Lost*—to praise its faults, but darkly, as occult successes[1]—and no one need suppose that criticism is going to disconcert them much. Still, if a calm and dispassionate witness can find some substance in the foregoing chapters, in praise and blame alike, their author will have no cause to regret them. I want to conclude with two more questions which, in rounding the matter off, any reasonable reader might be expected to take up.

The first may seem an academic question, yet it is to the purpose. In order to ask it one has to make a distinction between the style of the epic and the poet's artistic approach in general, but this procedure is less hazardous in the case of *Paradise Lost* than it might be with another poem. Can any connexion be found between the misjudgements in Milton's general handling of his material and the stylistic faults which show up when his verse is flagging? On the face of it the answer appears to be 'None'. Milton's general approach, when it errs, errs usually in the direction of particularity, of saying too much, of being too precise— whether about the properties of angels or the intentions of God— and no one would claim that this is a common weakness in his style. On the contrary, when his style is weak it is often because it is too vague, too unrealized. Some say that this is its chief virtue, that if it were more graphic it would be unreadable, but the argument has never seemed to me a strong one. When during the

---

[1] The interested reader may care to consult, as one example from an *embarras de choix*, the chapter on the War in Heaven in *Answerable Style*, by Arnold Stein (Minneapolis, 1953).

Creation the Son of God orders the waters to divide so that the land can appear, and they are described as being 'uprowld As drops on dust conglobing from the drie' (vii. 291-2), I find it impossible not to welcome the precision of the image. Would more images of the same sort really have spoiled the poem? It is hard to see what grounds there can be for supposing that they would.

In another way, however, some kind of connexion between the faults in the poet's broad approach and in his style does seem to discover itself. In his presentation of Heaven, and indeed in his presentation of the whole subject of his epic, Milton shows a distinct readiness to work on unfounded artistic assumptions, to take some things too easily for granted, and it is this as much as anything that robs the poem of its full share of conclusiveness. The bent can sometimes be seen in the minor details of his text—like the loose assertiveness of his statement that the angels received from God 'Beatitude past utterance' (iii. 62)—but more serious weaknesses can also be traced back to it. The crucial instance is his treatment of God. Clearly, Milton's underlying assumption about the figure of God is that it can be taken over intact from its context in the Bible or in Christian belief, and that there is little need to re-create it in the context of the poem. As clearly, this is imprudent. To accept the God of the poem the reader must first accept the assumption, interpreting the epic more as a vast biblical gloss than as a work of art complete and satisfying in itself; and if he jibs at doing so, trying to treat the poem correctly, as an artistic entity, God's characterization seems incomplete or downright bad. It is much as if a novelist were to retell the story of Hamlet and Ophelia, exaggerating all Hamlet's weaknesses and transferring all his virtues to Horatio, but relying on his reader's thorough knowledge of Shakespeare's play to save the prince from contumely. So too, though goodness knows the history of the Christian Church shows just how moot a case there is for it, Milton seems to feel that for God and Raphael to assert the doctrine of Free Will in their speeches is enough to win the reader's belief and trust in it, regardless of the other inferences which can be drawn from the behaviour of God or of Adam and Eve. This readiness to assume that certain ideas have been fully absorbed and integrated into the poem when they have not is roughly analogous to a common fault in the epic's style, a fault which is all too easy to exemplify:

His journies end and our beginning woe (iii. 633)

Hast thou turnd the least of these
To flight, or if to fall, but that they rise
Unvanquisht, easier to transact with mee
That thou shouldst hope, imperious, and with threats
To chase me hence? (vi. 284-8)

Aire, Water, Earth,
By Fowl, Fish, Beast, was flown, was swum, was walkt
Frequent (vii. 502-4)

Thoughts, which how found they harbour in thy brest
Adam, missthought of her to thee so dear? (ix. 288-9)

let him live
Before thee reconcil'd, at least his days
Numberd, though sad . . . . (xi. 38-40)

The same fault is incurred, much more absurdly, in Browning's version of the *Agamemnon*, a translation in which he acknowledges himself to have set literalism above all else, 'the very turn of each phrase in as Greek a fashion as English will bear':

Joy overcreeps me, calling forth the tear-drop.

But things there be, one barks,
When no man harks.

Such boast as this—of the veracious brimful—
Is not bad for a high-born dame to send forth.

And in my late-to-bed eyes damage have I . . . .

What, by the testifying "Ah me" of him,
Shall we prognosticate the man as perished?[1]

---

[1] *The Agamemnon of Aeschylus*, transcribed by Robert Browning (London, 1877), pp. v, 24, 38, 51, 71, 118.

Browning's idiosyncrasies of phrasing being very much his own the results are not the same, but the assumption underlying them is clearly very close to Milton's: that the idioms of another language, Greek, Latin, Hebrew—on rare occasions perhaps even of a hypothetical non-language—can be readily transposed into English and domesticated there. The assumption is that they will work as effectively in the English tongue as they do in their original. Yet surely to make any such assumption is very unwise. To borrow *words* from another tongue is a normal resource of poetry, indeed of language itself, and one which poets like Shakespeare and Milton (but Shakespeare in particular) quite properly exploit. Often it is through such exploitation that a word has entered the language in the first place, being subsequently adopted and legitimatized: 'castigate', 'militarist', 'eminence', &c. It is also an effective procedure to translate foreign idioms in dialogue, as Ernest Hemingway and other novelists have done in their novels, to show that a character is using another language and to give something of the flavour of his speech. This, however, is a different matter. Like Browning, Milton is deliberately subordinating the natural turn and grasp of English idiom to the idiom of other languages—usually highly inflected languages, where syntactical irregularities stand out much more recognisably than they can ever do in English—and the results sound strained and pedantic. They are sometimes misleading too, when words like 'unremov'd' (iv. 987), 'obvious' (vi. 69), 'discontinuous' (vi. 329), and 'securer' (ix. 371) are used in foreign and not in native senses.

  It would be foolish to maintain that the use of an artificial idiom is wholly bad. Milton's constructions often have the succinctness of classical syntax, a satisfying intricacy (i. 644-5, ii. 7-8, ii. 622-4, &c.), and some of them are the useful telescopings any poet is likely to seize on to condense his meaning. Compare—

> if aught propos'd
> And judg'd of public moment, in the shape
> Of difficulty or danger could deterr
> Mee from attempting.   (ii. 447-50)

—where 'aught' seems to be both the subject of 'could deterr' and the object of 'attempting', for example, with the compression in Yeats's injunction to the Duchess of Wellington, where 'ponder on' is both an imperative and the verb of an adjectival clause:

> Nothing that common women ponder on
> If you are worth my hope![1]

Again, the artificiality of Milton's syntax sometimes allows him to compass effects of great subtlety, like the suspended verb ('is . . . To be') which tactfully begs the question whether Earth has been created yet or not:

> There is a place
> (If ancient and prophetic fame in Heav'n
> Err not) another World, the happy seat
> Of some new Race call'd *Man*, about this time
> To be created like to us . . . .   (ii. 345-9)

But there are drawbacks to a style as synthetic as Milton's too, and to compare his syntax with Shakespeare's is to appreciate how serious they are. No one will claim that Shakespeare's syntax is not sometimes Latin—

> There be that can rule Naples
> As well as he that sleeps   (*Tempest*, II. i. 262-3)

or even Greek—

> Which is a wonder how his grace should glean it   (*Henry V*, I. i. 53)

but it would be absurd to pretend that such constructions are the norms of his style. Nearly always, under the opulent folds and flourishes of his verse, one can feel what Hopkins called the naked thew and sinew of the language flexing itself,[2] and even when he coins an idiom it is so in accord with the genius of the English tongue that it is readily absorbed into the resources of everyday speech: 'death by inches', 'seal the accuser's lips', 'do any man's

---

[1] 'To Dorothy Wellesley', *Last Poems and Plays* (London, 1940), p. 21.
[2] *The Letters of Gerard Manley Hopkins to Robert Bridges*, ed. C. C. Abbott (2nd edn., O.U.P., 1955), pp. 267-8.

heart good', &c. In *Paradise Lost* this is not so. Far from moulding itself to the curves and stresses of its native idiom the style of the epic stiffly preserves a foreign and unnatural cast, and the sacrifice in flexibility and vivacity is inordinate. Milton seems to use elliptical constructions, not to convey emotional disturbances or traits of character (as Shakespeare nearly always does), but as an end in themselves, for their formal patternings and the reminiscences of classical locutions they provide. The result is that his verse is disproportionately tortuous, with obscurities that seem accidental and pointless, and also that it is quite excessively verbal, more of a screening haze than a lucid medium. As Dr. Leavis has tellingly observed, 'He exhibits a feeling *for* words rather than a capacity for feeling *through* words', whereas in Shakespeare 'The total effect is as if words as words withdrew themselves from the focus of our attention and we were directly aware of a tissue of feelings and perceptions.'[1] Despite the successes they often permit, Milton's assumptions about the language of his poem are really no more desirable than his assumptions about the figure of God, and one can only agree with the verdict (ill-expressed, as Dr. Tillyard has shown, but instinctive and healthy) that Keats delivered on the epic's style. Especially by its poets, 'English ought to be kept up.'[2]

The second question that I want to raise, the last and the most important, is actually a complex of questions, some straight-forward and some not. If we ask why *Paradise Lost* should have maintained so high a reputation in spite of its defects it is easy enough to reply that this came about because previous generations were seemingly unable to distinguish, as we find it so easy to do, between God Himself and the God of the poem. But if we press the point, inquiring why this distinction eluded them, and why it no longer eludes ourselves, the answer will not come so pat. This is a very wide question indeed, and beyond saying that the critical advantage we now enjoy may not be entirely to our credit, that it

---

[1] *Revaluation* (London, 1936), pp. 48-9, 50.

[2] Letter to John Hamilton Reynolds, 21 September 1819. See *The Letters of John Keats*, ed. Maurice Buxton Forman (4th edn., O.U.P., 1952), p. 384, and E. M. W. Tillyard, *The Miltonic Setting* (London, 1947), pp. 105-14.

argues weaker convictions as well as clearer reading habits, I must be content simply to pose it, not to discuss it here. There is a simpler inquiry, directly related to this wide one, that is more germane to a critic's purpose, and I must deal with it less summarily. Granted that *Paradise Lost* is much less perfect than its apologists would have one believe, are its imperfections so disastrous as to deny it the status it has always had as one of the landmarks of our literature?

It is sometimes easy, when a critic is striving for precision of judgement about a poem of this order, to mistake his purpose for one of denigration. I can only hope that it has been made tolerably clear that I intend no such thing, that I have tried to trace the epic's successes and failures quite impartially, and that the attempt has done nothing to abate my regard for those successes which it can fairly claim. Nothing here written seems to me incompatible with such a regard, and indeed to have written at all presupposes it: one does not feel the urge to discriminate over *Davideis*, Blackmore's epics, or Young's *Night Thoughts*. That Milton's style falls short of the sustained enchantment of Shakespeare's, that it was unwise of him to regard his subject as 'sufficient of it self' (ix. 43), that much relating to God and to Heaven is flawed, and that an irreproachable but misplaced respect for the religion he championed has helped the flaws to pass unnoticed—these seem to me statements of fact, admissions that must be made. But *Paradise Lost* remains a poem for all to read and ponder, and this is especially the case in an age like our own, when Christianity is coming more and more to be regarded, not without daily pretext, as the bolthole of the neurotic, the diploma of the careerist, or the diversion of the aesthete. Indeed for an age like the present, an age of anxiety, the epic's value may stem more from its flaws than its merits. The tenets of Christianity, of any sustaining Faith, are hopes and inquiries phrased as affirmations, and merely to rephrase them, as a successful *Paradise Lost* would have done, cannot advance them much. One virtue of the imperfect poem we have is that it incites us to think more purposefully about these hopes and inquiries, about matters which (to put them no higher) are of deep concern to us all. If we bring to the poem the attention it merits, free of all preconceptions, it cannot fail to stimulate our religious thinking as few other poems still can do.

Finally, for those who find this too negative, the positives remain: Satan's early appearances, the Garden, the Fall, the sudden soarings in the verse, and the moving celebration of Man's spirit— all the more moving when we remember (as who can forget?) that it was the song of a man in his blindness, forlorn and perhaps disliked. Modern criticism tends to forget, what Aristotle for one did not,[1] that size itself is an aesthetic quality, a prime factor among those determining our assessment of a work of art. Flaws count, of course; but how much they count depends less on their weight than their specific gravity, the ratio they bear to size, to mass and extent. *Paradise Lost* has an historical claim to our attention that is as high as that of the plays of Shakespeare. Its aesthetic claim is lower, I believe appreciably lower, but it is firm and secure. A writer's faults are the price we must pay for his triumphs, for what he has won. Weighed in that balance Milton's will not seem exorbitant, though they are there.

---

[1] *Poetics* 5. 1449^b 25; cf. 7. 1450^b 24-5.

APPENDIX

For those who may be interested, the original Dutch text of the passages translated from Vondel in Chapter One and Chapter Three are given here:

A. *Eva:* Zoo lang het aerdtrijck in den arm des hemels hangt,
En d' aerde, zijne bruit, haer vruchtbaerheit ontfangt
Van zulck een' bruidegom, die haer met duizent oogen
Van starren aenlonckt, en bestraelt uit 's hemels boogen,
Zoo lang zal mijne min met d' uwe gaen gepaert,
En elcke dienst en kus blijft my een' weêrkus waert.

   Adam: Het zy met uw verlof, dat ick in deze streecke,
Aen d' eene zijde, een poos met Godt den schepper
       spreecke,
En in mijne eenzaemheit bedanck' voor uw genot.
Verschoonme een' oogenblick.
                       (*Adam in Ballingschap*, 1022-31)

B. *Eva:* De goddelijcke galm van 't heiligh bruiloftsliet
Ontknoopt den bant, die ziel en lichaem hiel gebonden.
De ziel, op hemelscheit verslingert, en verslonden,
Gevoelt geene aerdtscheit, en, verkeert in zuivre vlam,
Zoeckt d' eerste bron, waeruit zy haeren oirsprong nam.

   Adam: Mijn lief, waer heene? toef: gy mostme niet ontzweeven.

   Eva: Ick worde krachtigh na de bron des heils gedreven,
Die mijnen brant alleen kan koelen. laetme gaen.

   Adam: Uw element is hier. uw liefste spreeckt u aen.

   Eva: Nu kome ick weder tot my zelve, en by mijn zinnen.
                       (*Adam in Ballingschap*, 935-44)

M

C.   Ghy vat het recht: het past rechtschape heerschappyen
      Geensins hun wettigheit zoo los te laten glyen:
      Want d' oppermaght is d' eerste aen hare wet verplicht;
      Verandren voeght haer minst. ben ick een zoon van 't
          licht,
      Een heerscher over 't licht, ick zal mijn Recht bewaren:
      Ick zwicht voor geen gewelt, noch aertsgeweldenaren.
      Laet zwichten al wat wil: ick wijck niet eenen voet.
      Hier is myn Vaderlant. noch ramp, noch tegenspoet,
      Noch vloecken zullen ons vervaren, noch betoomen.
      Wy zullen sneven, of dien hoeck te boven komen.
      Is 't noodlot dat ick vall', van eere en staet berooft:
      Laet vallen, als ick vall' met deze kroone op 't hooft,
      Dien scepter in de vuist, dien eersleip van vertrouden,
      En zoo veel duizenden als onze zyde houden.
      Dat vallen streckt tot eer, en onverwelckbren lof.
      En liever d' eerste Vorst in eenigh lager hof,
      Dan in 't gezalight licht de tweede, of noch een minder.
      Zoo troost ick my de kans, en vrees nu leet noch hinder.
                                                    (*Lucifer*, 428-45)

D.   Zoo wort mijn wraeck verzaet. nu triomfeert de hel.
      Dat mijn erfvyant zich nu weere, en wetten stell',
      Om zulck eene inbreuck van erflasteren te keeren:
      Wy passen langer op geen' hinderdam noch beeren
      Van wetten, en belofte, en vreeslijck dreigement.
      Natuur leght onder, plat getreden, en geschent.
      Al 't menschelijck geslacht is mijn, en errefeigen.
      Het past niet langer op beloften, noch op dreigen.
      De wil helt over van 't geboden goet tot quaet.
      'k Wil kercken zaeien, en altaeren, hem ten smaet.
      Men zal mijn beelden daer met menschenoffren eeren,
      En gout en wieroock, en by 's afgronts godtheit
          zweeren,
      Uit schrick voor straffe. ick schuif nu glimpelijck en
          valsch

Den oirsprong van het quaet van my op 's vyants hals.
Laet al de weerelt vry van Adams erven krielen:
Uit sestigh eeuwen berght hy pas een hantvol zielen.
Zoo stijge ick, na mijn' val, op eenen hooger trap.
Zoo veel vermagh de lust, een montvol appelsap.

(Adam in Ballingschap, 1460-77)

Reliable English translations of both *Lucifer* and *Adam in Ballingschap* are to be found in *The Celestial Cycle* by Watson Kirkconnell (Toronto, 1952), together with some comments on Milton's possible debt to Vondel. Dr. Kirkconnell is wisely sceptical about the extent of such a debt, but even to prove conclusively that it was owed is very difficult. A translator can easily render the two lines in passage C above,

> En liever d' eerste Vorst in eenigh lager hof,
> Dan in 't gezalight licht de tweede, of noch een minder,

so that they closely resemble Milton's 'Better to reign in Hell, then serve in Heav'n' (i. 263), following the same procedure with other passages, and if he does so Vondel's influence on *Paradise Lost* will seem beyond dispute. This was apparently the method of George Edmundson in his *Milton and Vondel* (London, 1885), a book to which, despite their understandable temptation to do otherwise, even Dutch scholars have taken exception.[1] Let the translator take care to avoid Miltonic echoes, however, and Vondel's influence, for all its general probability, will seem remote. That is the problem, and since two distinct languages are involved it seems to me insoluble on the basis of the texts alone. Other evidence is needed, but to date it is hopelessly flimsy.

---

[1] See, for example, J. J. Moolhuizen, *Vondels Lucifer en Miltons Verloren Paradijs* (The Hague, 1895).

INDEX